C++ Game Development

Build High-Performance Games from Scratch

JARREL E.

Contents

Foreword   vi

Preface   vii

Acknowledgement   viii

I   Foundations of C++ Game Development

Introduction to Game Development with C++   3

    Getting Started with Game Development in C++   4

    Understanding the Basics of Game Development   5

    Why Choose C++ for Game Development   7

    Overview of Game Development Tools and Frameworks   9

Setting Up Your Development Environment   12

    Installing C++ Compiler and IDE   12

    Configuring Graphics Libraries   14

    Setting Up Game Assets and Resources   15

Fundamentals of Game Design   20

    Game Design Principles and Concepts   20

    Creating Game Mechanics and Rules   22

    Prototyping Your Game Ideas   25

Getting Started with C++ Game Programming   30

    Understanding C++ Basics   31

    Introduction to Object-Oriented Programming   33

    Working with Data Structures in C++ and Algorithms   37

II   Advanced Topics and Project Development

Advanced Topics in C++ Game Development   43
  Shader Programming with GLSL   43
    Advanced Graphics Techniques   50
      Integrating Third-Party Libraries and SDKs   69
Case Studies and Game Development Projects   72
  Building a Simple 2D Platformer Game   72
    Developing a 3D First-Person Shooter   82
      Creating a Multiplayer Online Battle Arena (MOBA) Game   91
Conclusion and Next Steps   95
  Recap of Key Learnings   95
    Further Resources for Game Development   97
      Next Steps in Your Game Development Journey   98

III   Core Game Development Techniques

Graphics Rendering with OpenGL   103
  Introduction to OpenGL   104
    Setting Up OpenGL Environment   106
      Rendering 2D and 3D Graphics   110
Game Physics and Collision Detection   114
  Implementing Physics in Games   115
    Understanding Collision Detection Algorithms   117
      Integrating Physics Engine into Your Game   122
  Example Code for Creating Box2D Bodies: 123
Audio and Sound Effects   125
  Introduction to Game Audio   126
    Implementing Sound Effects in C++   128
      Managing Audio Assets and Mixing   130
User Input and Controls   133
  Handling Keyboard and Mouse Input   134
    Implementing Gamepad Support   137

Touchscreen and Mobile Input Integration ... 140

Game AI and Pathfinding ... 143

Introduction to Artificial Intelligence in Games ... 144

Implementing Basic AI Behaviors ... 147

Pathfinding Algorithms for Game Characters ... 150

Networking and Multiplayer ... 154

Introduction to Network Programming ... 155

Implementing Multiplayer Support in C++ ... 160

Server-Client Architecture for Online Games ... 165

Optimization Techniques for High-Performance ... 171

Profiling and Performance Analysis ... 172

Memory Management Best Practices ... 174

Optimizing Graphics and Rendering Pipeline ... 176

Testing, Debugging, and Deployment ... 179

Strategies for Testing Game Code ... 180

Debugging Techniques for C++ Games ... 181

Deploying Your Game on Multiple Platforms ... 183

Sample Game Project ... 185

References ... 191

About the Author ... 192

Also by Jarrel E. ... 193

Foreword

Welcome to the exhilarating world of C++ Game Development! In this dynamic and immersive journey, you'll embark on an exciting adventure into the realm of game creation, armed with the powerful tools and techniques of the C++ programming language. Whether you're a seasoned developer looking to expand your skill set or a newcomer eager to dive into the captivating realm of game design, this book is your essential companion on the path to mastering the art of game development.

Within these pages, you'll discover a treasure trove of knowledge, insights, and hands-on tutorials that will equip you with the expertise needed to bring your gaming visions to life. From the fundamental principles of game programming to advanced techniques in graphics rendering, physics simulation, and multiplayer networking, each chapter offers a comprehensive exploration of key concepts, accompanied by practical examples and real-world applications.

With a focus on practicality and creativity, this book empowers you to unleash your imagination and transform your ideas into captivating gaming experiences. Whether you dream of crafting epic adventures, fast-paced action thrillers, or mind-bending puzzle games, the skills and techniques presented here will empower you to turn your dreams into reality.

Now grab your keyboard, fire up your IDE, and get ready to go on an exciting adventure into the core of C++ game development. Now let's get the adventure started!

Preface

Enter the thrilling universe of C++ Game Development—a realm where imagination melds seamlessly with cutting-edge technology, and the boundaries of what's possible are constantly pushed to new heights. In this exhilarating journey, you are invited to embark on an odyssey of creativity, innovation, and endless possibilities.

Gaming has evolved from a mere pastime to a cultural phenomenon that captivates hearts and minds across the globe. Behind every mesmerizing game lies a team of visionary developers who bring dreams to life through lines of code and pixels on a screen. Now, it's your turn to step into the spotlight and unleash your creativity upon the world.

Within the pages of this book, you will discover a treasure trove of knowledge and insights meticulously crafted to empower you on your quest for game development mastery. From the thrill of crafting immersive worlds to the satisfaction of overcoming technical challenges, each chapter is designed to fuel your passion and propel you toward greatness.

But this is more than just a book—it's your ticket to adventure, your roadmap to success, and your guide through the exhilarating landscape of game development. So, brace yourself for an epic journey filled with twists, turns, and moments of pure exhilaration. The world of C++ Game Development awaits.

Acknowledgement

This book would not have been possible without the contributions, support, and encouragement of countless individuals who have lent their expertise, insights, and inspiration along the way.

First and foremost, I would like to express my deepest gratitude to Ethan Reynolds, whose unwavering guidance and mentorship have been invaluable throughout this journey. Their wisdom, patience, and encouragement have shaped this book into what it is today.

I am also immensely grateful to Emma Martinez, Olivia Chang, and Noah Thompson for their tireless efforts in reviewing and providing feedback on the manuscript. Their keen insights and attention to detail have helped refine the content and ensure its accuracy and relevance.

I extend my heartfelt thanks to the entire team at Quantum Publishing, whose dedication and professionalism have made the publication of this book a reality. From editing and design to marketing and distribution, their support has been instrumental every step of the way.

Last but not least, I would like to thank my family and friends for their unwavering love, encouragement, and understanding throughout the ups and downs of this journey. Their support has been the driving force behind my passion for game development and the inspiration behind every word written in these pages.

To all those who have played a part in bringing this book to life, thank you from the bottom of my heart. Your contributions have made a difference, and I am forever grateful for your support.

I

Foundations of C++ Game Development

Introduction to Game Development with C++

Game development is an exciting and rewarding field that combines creativity, problem-solving, and technical skills. C++ is a powerful and versatile programming language that has been widely used in the game development industry for decades. In this introduction, we will explore the fundamentals of game development with C++ and provide you with a solid foundation to start your journey.

Why C++ for Game Development?

C++ is a popular choice for game development due to its performance, flexibility, and low-level control over hardware. It allows developers to optimize code for maximum efficiency, which is crucial in the fast-paced and resource-intensive world of game development. Additionally, C++ provides access to powerful libraries and frameworks that simplify the development process and enable the creation of complex and visually stunning games.

Key Concepts in Game Development with C++

Game Engines: Game engines are software frameworks that provide a comprehensive set of tools and features for building games. Popular C++ game engines include Unreal Engine, Unity, and Cocos2D-x. These engines handle tasks such as rendering, input handling, physics simulation, and asset management, allowing developers to focus on the game's logic and design.

Graphics Programming: C++ provides low-level access to graphics APIs like OpenGL and DirectX, enabling developers to create high-performance, visually stunning graphics for their games. This includes techniques such as 3D rendering, texture mapping, and shader programming.

Game Loops and Event Handling: The game loop is the core of a game's logic, responsible for continuously updating the game state and rendering the game world. C++ allows for precise control over the game loop, ensuring smooth and responsive gameplay.

Data Structures and Algorithms: Efficient data structures and algorithms are crucial in game development, as they help manage large amounts of game data and perform complex calculations quickly. C++ provides a wide range of data structures, such as arrays, linked lists, and hash tables, as well as powerful algorithms for tasks like pathfinding and collision detection.

Networking and Multiplayer: C++ is well-suited for developing networked and multiplayer games, thanks to its support for low-level network programming and the availability of libraries like Boost.Asio and SFML.Network.

Memory Management: C++'s manual memory management, through the use of pointers and dynamic memory allocation, allows developers to optimize memory usage and performance, which is essential in resource-constrained game environments.

Getting Started with Game Development in C++

To begin your journey in game development with C++, you'll need to familiarize yourself with the following:

- **C++ Programming Fundamentals**: Ensure you have a solid understanding of C++ syntax, data types, control structures, and object-oriented programming concepts.
- **Game Development Frameworks and Libraries**: Explore popular C++ game engines and libraries, such as Unreal Engine, Unity, SFML, and Cocos2D-x, to understand their features and capabilities.
- **Graphics Programming**: Learn about 2D and 3D graphics programming, including topics like rendering, texture mapping, and shader programming.
- **Game Loop and Event Handling**: Understand the game loop structure and how to handle user input and other game events effectively.
- **Data Structures and Algorithms**: Study common data structures and algorithms used in game development, such as arrays, linked lists, and pathfinding algorithms.
- **Networking and Multiplayer**: Familiarize yourself with network programming concepts and libraries for developing networked and multiplayer games.
- **Game Design and Project Management**: Develop an understanding of game design principles and project management techniques to create successful game projects.

All these concepts will be demonstrated later in this book. Remember, game development is a continuous learning process, so be prepared to explore, experiment, and continuously expand your knowledge and skills.

Understanding the Basics of Game Development

At its core, game programming revolves around the implementation of gameplay mechanics, systems, and features that define the interactive elements of a game. Whether it's controlling character movement, simulating physics interactions, or managing player input, game programming is responsible for translating game design concepts into functional code.

Central to the fundamentals of game programming is a deep understanding of computer science principles, particularly data structures, algorithms, and software design patterns. Data structures such as arrays, lists, and trees are used to organize and manipulate game data, while algorithms govern the behavior of game objects, handle collision detection, and manage game state transitions.

Equally important is proficiency in programming languages commonly used in game development, with C++ standing out as a preferred choice due to its performance, flexibility, and widespread adoption in the industry. Mastery of C++ allows game programmers to leverage its powerful features, such as object-oriented programming, memory management, and low-level system access, to optimize game performance and achieve complex gameplay mechanics.

Beyond the technical aspects, game programming also requires a strong grasp of game design principles and player psychology. By understanding player motivations, preferences, and behaviors, game programmers can tailor gameplay experiences to maximize engagement and enjoyment. This often involves collaborating closely with game designers and artists to implement features that enhance immersion, challenge players, and evoke emotional responses.

One of the key challenges in game programming is optimizing performance to ensure smooth, responsive gameplay across a variety of hardware platforms. This involves minimizing computational overhead, optimizing memory usage, and leveraging hardware-accelerated graphics and audio APIs to maximize efficiency. Profiling and performance analysis tools are used to identify bottlenecks and areas for improvement, allowing developers to fine-tune their code for optimal performance.

Another critical aspect of game programming is managing complexity and maintaining code scalability and reusability. As games grow in scope and complexity, maintaining a clean, modular codebase becomes increasingly important to facilitate collaboration, facilitate code maintenance, and support future expansions and updates. Software design patterns such as the entity-component-system (ECS) architecture and the model-view-controller (MVC) pattern are commonly employed to organize code and promote code reuse and flexibility.

In addition to technical skills, effective communication and collaboration are essential qualities for game programmers. Working closely with artists, designers, and other team members, game programmers must be able to translate design concepts into actionable code, solicit feedback, and iterate on their implementations to achieve the desired gameplay experience.

Ultimately, the fundamentals of game programming represent a fusion of art and science, where creativity meets technical prowess to create interactive experiences that captivate and inspire players. By mastering the core principles of game programming, aspiring developers can embark on a journey of exploration and innovation, where every line of code brings them one step closer to realizing their creative vision in the digital realm.

Why Choose C++ for Game Development

Selecting the right programming language for game development is crucial, as it directly impacts performance, flexibility, and the overall development process. C++ stands out as a top choice for game development due to several compelling reasons:

- **Performance**: C++ is renowned for its high performance and efficiency. It provides direct access to hardware resources and allows for fine-grained control over memory management, making it well-suited for developing performance-critical applications like games. By leveraging features such as pointers, manual memory allocation, and inline assembly, developers can optimize code to achieve maximum speed and efficiency, crucial for demanding real-time applications like games.

- **Cross-Platform Compatibility**: C++ offers excellent cross-platform compatibility, allowing developers to write code that can be compiled and run on various operating systems and hardware platforms without major modifications. This makes it easier to target multiple platforms, including desktop computers, consoles, mobile devices, and even embedded systems, maximizing the reach and potential audience of the game.

- **Industry Standard**: C++ has been a staple in the game development industry for decades and remains widely used today. Many game engines, middleware, and development tools are built using C++ or provide robust support for it, making it a natural choice for developers looking to work with established frameworks and technologies. Additionally, a wealth of resources, tutorials, and community support is available for C++, making it easier for developers to learn and master the language.

- **Control and Flexibility**: C++ offers developers unparalleled control and flexibility over the development process. Its low-level nature allows for direct manipulation of hardware resources and efficient implementation of complex algorithms and data structures, empowering developers to create highly optimized and customizable game engines and systems. This level of control is essential for achieving the performance, scalability, and unique features required by modern games.

- **Integration with Existing Libraries and Tools**: C++ seamlessly integrates with a vast ecosystem of libraries, APIs, and tools commonly used in game development. From graphics libraries like OpenGL and DirectX to physics engines like Bullet and Box2D, C++ provides native support for interfacing with external libraries and leveraging existing solutions to accelerate development. This allows developers to focus on implementing game-specific features rather than reinventing the wheel.

- **Legacy Support**: Many legacy game engines and codebases are written in C++, making it essential for maintaining and extending existing projects. By learning C++, developers can tap into a wealth of job opportunities and contribute to a wide range of projects across the gaming industry, from indie games to AAA titles.

C++ offers a winning combination of performance, cross-platform compatibility, industry support, control, flexibility, and integration capabilities, making it the preferred choice for game developers seeking to create high-quality, high-performance games that push the boundaries of technology and immersion.

Overview of Game Development Tools and Frameworks

Game development tools and frameworks play a pivotal role in shaping the development process and determining the success of a project. By leveraging the right tools and frameworks, developers can streamline workflow, optimize performance, and unleash their creative potential to create memorable and engaging gaming experiences. Whether it's choosing a game engine, selecting an IDE, or integrating middleware and libraries, careful consideration of tools and frameworks is essential for realizing the vision of a game and bringing it to fruition.

This overview explores a variety of game development tools and frameworks that cater to different needs and preferences, offering insights into their features, capabilities, and suitability for various types of projects.

Game Engines:

- **Unity**: Unity is a popular and versatile game engine known for its user-friendly interface, cross-platform support, and extensive asset store. It offers a wide range of features, including 2D and 3D rendering, physics simulation, AI scripting, and multiplayer networking, making it suitable for projects of all sizes and genres.
- **Unreal Engine**: Unreal Engine is a powerful and feature-rich game engine renowned for its high-fidelity graphics, advanced rendering capabilities, and robust toolset. It provides a comprehensive suite of tools for creating immersive experiences, including visual scripting, animation, audio editing, and virtual reality support, making it a top choice for AAA game

development.

- **Godot Engine**: Godot Engine is a free and open-source game engine that offers a lightweight yet powerful alternative to commercial engines. It features a modular architecture, intuitive scripting language, and extensive documentation, making it accessible to developers of all skill levels. Godot supports both 2D and 3D game development and provides built-in tools for animation, physics simulation, and scene management.
- **CRYENGINE**: CRYENGINE is a cutting-edge game engine known for its stunning visuals, real-time rendering capabilities, and advanced physics simulation. It is favored by developers for creating visually impressive games with realistic graphics and dynamic environments. CRYENGINE offers a range of features, including procedural generation, particle effects, and advanced lighting and shading techniques.

Integrated Development Environments (IDEs):

- **Visual Studio**: Visual Studio is a powerful and feature-rich IDE widely used for C++ game development. It provides a comprehensive set of tools for code editing, debugging, profiling, and version control, as well as seamless integration with popular game engines and frameworks. Visual Studio offers a customizable user interface, extensive plugin ecosystem, and support for a wide range of programming languages and platforms.
- **JetBrains CLion**: CLion is a cross-platform C++ IDE designed for professional developers. It offers advanced code analysis, refactoring tools, and intelligent code completion, making it ideal for large-scale game projects. CLion provides seamless integration with CMake, the de facto standard build system for C++ projects, as well as support for version control systems like Git and Mercurial.
- **Xcode**: Xcode is the official IDE for macOS and iOS development, offering a comprehensive suite of tools for creating games and applications for Apple platforms. It features a streamlined workflow, built-in support for Swift and Objective-C programming languages, and powerful debugging and testing capabilities. Xcode also includes a visual editor for designing

user interfaces and layout constraints, making it easy to create responsive and visually appealing games for iOS and macOS devices.

Middleware and Libraries:

- **FMOD Studio**: FMOD Studio is a professional-grade audio middleware solution used by game developers to create interactive and immersive soundscapes. It offers a range of features, including real-time mixing, dynamic DSP effects, and multiplatform support, making it ideal for games with complex audio requirements.
- **PhysX**: PhysX is a real-time physics simulation engine developed by NVIDIA, widely used in game development for simulating realistic physical interactions and effects. It provides a robust physics engine, advanced collision detection, and support for hardware acceleration, enabling developers to create lifelike animations, destructible environments, and dynamic gameplay mechanics.
- **SDL (Simple DirectMedia Layer)**: SDL is a cross-platform multimedia library used for creating games and multimedia applications. It provides low-level access to audio, keyboard, mouse, and graphics hardware, making it suitable for developing games that require precise control over input and output. SDL offers support for multiple platforms, including Windows, macOS, Linux, iOS, and Android, making it a versatile choice for cross-platform game development.

Setting Up Your Development Environment

Setting up your development environment for C++ game development is essential to kickstart your project efficiently. Here's a concise guide to get you started:

1. Install a C++ Compiler and IDE: Choose a C++ compiler such as GCC, Clang, or Microsoft Visual C++ Compiler, and an Integrated Development Environment (IDE) like Visual Studio, CLion, or Code::Blocks.
2. Configure Graphics Libraries: Set up graphics libraries like OpenGL or DirectX for rendering graphics in your game. Install necessary drivers and dependencies to ensure smooth graphics performance.
3. Acquire Game Assets and Resources: Gather game assets such as sprites, textures, audio files, and 3D models from reliable sources or create them yourself using tools like Blender, GIMP, or Audacity.

With these steps completed, you'll have a solid foundation for embarking on your C++ game development journey. Let's expound on these steps.

Installing C++ Compiler and IDE

To begin your C++ game development journey, you'll need to install a C++ compiler and an Integrated Development Environment (IDE). Here's a simple guide to get you started:

Install a C++ Compiler: Choose a C++ compiler suitable for your operating system:

- For Windows: You can install Microsoft Visual C++ Compiler by downloading and installing Visual Studio Community edition from the official Microsoft website.
- For macOS: Xcode comes with the Clang compiler, which supports C++ development. Install Xcode from the Mac App Store.
- For Linux: You can install GCC (GNU Compiler Collection), which includes the G++ C++ compiler. Use your package manager to install GCC, such as apt for Ubuntu or yum for CentOS.

Install an Integrated Development Environment (IDE): Choose an IDE that suits your preferences and needs:

- Visual Studio: A powerful IDE available on Windows, offering comprehensive features for C++ development, including debugging, code navigation, and project management.
- CLion: A cross-platform IDE developed by JetBrains, providing intelligent code completion, refactoring tools, and seamless integration with CMake.
- Code::Blocks: A lightweight and customizable IDE available on Windows, macOS, and Linux, offering a simple interface and support for multiple compilers.
- Xcode: The official IDE for macOS and iOS development, offering a streamlined workflow and advanced debugging tools for C++ development.

Once you've installed the compiler and IDE of your choice, you'll be ready to start coding your C++ games but first let's configure the graphic libraries.

Configuring Graphics Libraries

Graphics libraries, also known as graphics APIs (Application Programming Interfaces), are software libraries or frameworks that provide developers with a set of functions and tools for rendering graphics in computer programs, including games, simulations, and graphical applications. These libraries abstract the complexities of interacting with graphics hardware and provide developers with a higher-level interface for creating and manipulating graphical elements.

Configuring graphics libraries is essential for rendering graphics in your C++ game development projects. Here's a brief guide to get you started:

Choose a Graphics Library: Decide which graphics library you want to use based on your project requirements and platform compatibility. Common choices include:

- OpenGL: A cross-platform graphics API widely used for rendering 2D and 3D graphics. It provides low-level access to the GPU and is supported on Windows, macOS, Linux, and mobile platforms.
- DirectX: Developed by Microsoft, DirectX is primarily used for game development on Windows platforms. It provides high-level abstractions for rendering graphics, audio, and input.
- Vulkan: A modern graphics API designed for high-performance, low-overhead rendering. Vulkan offers more control and flexibility compared to OpenGL but requires more effort to use effectively.

Install Graphics Drivers: Ensure that your graphics drivers are up to date, especially if you're using OpenGL or DirectX. Visit the website of your graphics card manufacturer (NVIDIA, AMD, or Intel) to download and install the latest drivers for your GPU.

Set Up Development Environment: Depending on the chosen graphics library, you may need to configure your development environment:

- For OpenGL: Include the OpenGL headers in your project and link against the OpenGL library. On Windows, you may need to use a library loader like GLEW (OpenGL Extension Wrangler Library) or GLAD (OpenGL Loader Generator) to access OpenGL functions.
- For DirectX: Install the DirectX SDK (Software Development Kit) if you're targeting older versions of DirectX (prior to DirectX 12). If you're using DirectX 12, ensure that you have the appropriate Windows SDK installed.

Initialize Graphics Context: In your C++ code, initialize the graphics context using the chosen library. For example:

- For OpenGL: Create an OpenGL context using platform-specific APIs like GLFW, SDL, or SFML. Initialize OpenGL functions using the library loader.
- For DirectX: Initialize the DirectX graphics device and swap chain, and create a rendering context using the DirectX API.

Test Graphics Rendering: Write a simple graphics rendering program to test that your configuration is working correctly. Render basic shapes or load a simple 3D model to verify that graphics are being displayed as expected.

By following these steps, you can configure graphics libraries for your C++ game development projects and start rendering graphics with ease.

Setting Up Game Assets and Resources

Game assets and resources refer to the various elements used in the creation of a video game, ranging from graphical elements to audio files and beyond. These assets are essential components that contribute to the overall look, feel, and functionality of the game. Here's a breakdown of the different types of game assets and resources:

Graphics: Graphics encompass visual elements such as:

- Sprites: 2D images representing characters, objects, and animations.
- Textures: Images applied to 3D models to add detail and color.
- Backgrounds: Images or scenes that form the backdrop of game levels or environments.
- User Interface (UI) Elements: Buttons, menus, icons, and other graphical elements used for user interaction.

Audio: Audio assets include various sound files used to enhance the auditory experience of the game:

- Music: Background music tracks that set the mood and atmosphere of the game.
- Sound Effects: Short audio clips used to represent actions, events, and interactions within the game (e.g., footsteps, explosions, gunfire).
- Voiceovers: Recorded dialogue or narration used for storytelling, character dialogue, or tutorials.

3D Models: 3D models are used to represent characters, objects, and environments in three-dimensional space:

- Characters: Playable characters, non-playable characters (NPCs), enemies, and creatures.
- Props: Interactive objects, items, and environmental elements.
- Environments: Buildings, landscapes, terrain, and architectural structures.

Animations: Animations bring game elements to life by adding movement and dynamics:

- Character Animations: Sequences of movements and actions for characters (e.g., walking, running, jumping, attacking).

- Object Animations: Dynamic animations for objects, effects, and environmental elements (e.g., doors opening, explosions, weather effects).
- UI Animations: Animated transitions, effects, and feedback within the user interface (e.g., button presses, menu transitions).

Text and Fonts: Text assets include in-game text, dialogue, and user interface elements:

- Game Text: On-screen text for menus, instructions, tutorials, and subtitles.
- Fonts: Typeface styles used for displaying text in the game, chosen to match the game's visual style and theme.

Level Design Elements: Level design assets are used to create game levels, environments, and scenarios:

- Tilesets: Sets of tiles used to construct game levels, environments, and backgrounds.
- Props and Decorations: Environmental elements, obstacles, and decorative objects placed within game levels.
- Level Layouts: Blueprints or layouts outlining the structure, layout, and flow of game levels.

These are just a few examples of the many types of assets and resources used in game development. Each asset contributes to the overall gameplay experience, helping to create immersive worlds, engaging narratives, and memorable gaming experiences for players.

Setting up game assets and resources is a crucial step in the game development process, ensuring that you have all the necessary elements to bring your game to life. Here's a concise guide to setting up game assets and resources:

Define Game Requirements: Identify the types of assets and resources your game will need, such as graphics, audio, 3D models, animations, textures, fonts, and level design elements.

Acquire or Create Assets: Obtain game assets from reliable sources or create them yourself using specialized software tools. This may include:

- Graphics: Sprites, textures, backgrounds, icons, and user interface elements. You can create graphics using tools like Adobe Photoshop, GIMP, or Aseprite.
- Audio: Music tracks, sound effects, voiceovers, and ambient sounds. You can create audio assets using software like Audacity, FL Studio, or Logic Pro.
- 3D Models: Characters, props, environments, and objects. Use 3D modeling software like Blender, Autodesk Maya, or 3ds Max to create 3D models.
- Animations: Animated sprites, character animations, and particle effects. Tools like Spine, DragonBones, or Unity's animation system can help create animations.
- Textures: Textures for 3D models and environments. Create or edit textures using software like Substance Painter, Photoshop, or GIMP.
- Fonts: Choose fonts that match the visual style and theme of your game. Websites like Google Fonts or Adobe Fonts offer a wide selection of free and paid fonts.

Organize Assets: Organize your assets into a structured directory hierarchy within your project folder. Create separate folders for each asset type (e.g., "Graphics", "Audio", "Models") to keep your project organized and maintainable.

Optimize Assets: Optimize your assets for performance and efficiency. This may involve reducing file sizes, optimizing image compression, and minimizing audio file sizes without sacrificing quality. Use tools like ImageOptim, Audacity, or Adobe Media Encoder to optimize assets.

Import Assets into Game Engine: Import your assets into your game development environment or game engine. Most game engines provide built-in tools or importers for various asset types, allowing you to easily import and manage assets within your project.

Test Assets: Test your assets within the game engine to ensure they are working as intended and integrate seamlessly with your game mechanics and systems. Make any necessary adjustments or refinements based on feedback and testing results.

By following these steps, you can set up game assets and resources effectively, laying the groundwork for the development of your game. With a comprehensive collection of assets at your disposal, you'll be well-equipped to bring your game vision to fruition.

Fundamentals of Game Design

The fundamentals of game design encompass the core principles and concepts that guide the creation of interactive experiences for players. Game design is a multidisciplinary field that draws upon elements of psychology, storytelling, user experience, and game mechanics to craft engaging and immersive games.

Game Design Principles and Concepts

Game design principles and concepts form the foundation upon which engaging and immersive games are built. These principles guide designers in creating experiences that captivate players and keep them coming back for more. Here's an overview of some key game design principles and concepts:

Clear Goals and Objectives: Games should provide clear goals and objectives for players to strive towards. Whether it's completing a level, defeating an opponent, or achieving a high score, clear objectives give players a sense of purpose and direction.

Meaningful Choices: Meaningful choices empower players to shape their own experience and influence the outcome of the game. Choices should have consequences that impact gameplay, story progression, or character development, creating a sense of agency and ownership.

Balanced Challenge: Games should offer a balanced level of challenge that is neither too easy nor too difficult. Balancing challenge ensures that players are appropriately challenged without feeling frustrated or bored, maintaining engagement and motivation.

Reward Systems: Reward systems provide positive reinforcement for player actions and accomplishments. Rewards can take many forms, including points, power-ups, unlockable content, and in-game currency, incentivizing players to progress and explore.

Progression Systems: Progression systems track player advancement and provide a sense of accomplishment as players overcome challenges and achieve milestones. Progression can be linear, branching, or open-ended, offering different paths for players to explore.

Feedback and Iteration: Feedback mechanisms provide players with immediate and informative feedback on their actions and decisions. Feedback can take the form of visual, auditory, or tactile cues, reinforcing desired behaviors and guiding player learning and skill development.

Immersion and Atmosphere: Immersion and atmosphere draw players into the game world and make the experience more compelling and believable. Immersive elements include realistic graphics, immersive sound design, compelling storytelling, and attention to detail.

Player Empowerment: Player empowerment gives players a sense of agency and control over their experience. Empowerment can come from player customization options, skill-based gameplay mechanics, and opportunities for player expression and creativity.

Accessibility and Inclusivity: Games should be accessible and inclusive to players of all abilities, backgrounds, and preferences. Designing for accessibility involves considering factors such as difficulty settings, customizable controls, and inclusive representation in game content.

Emergent Gameplay: Emergent gameplay arises from the interaction of game systems and player choices, resulting in unexpected and dynamic gameplay experiences. Designing for emergent gameplay encourages creativity, experimentation, and replayability.

Game design principles and concepts are the foundational elements that guide the creation of engaging and immersive games. By incorporating these principles into game design, developers can create experiences that captivate players and keep them coming back for more.

Creating Game Mechanics and Rules

Creating game mechanics and rules involves defining the interactive systems and rules that govern player actions, behaviors, and outcomes within a game. Let's explore some key concepts and how they can be implemented using C++ code where applicable:

layer Movement:

- Define player movement mechanics such as walking, running, jumping, and crouching.
- Implement movement controls using keyboard, mouse, or gamepad inputs.

```cpp
// Example C++ code for player movement
if (isKeyPressed(KEY_UP_ARROW)) {
    player.moveForward();
}
if (isKeyPressed(KEY_DOWN_ARROW)) {
    player.moveBackward();
}
// Similar implementations for other movement directions
```

Collision Detection:

- Implement collision detection to detect when game objects intersect or collide with each other.
- Handle collision responses such as player-enemy collisions or player-object interactions.

```cpp
// Example C++ code for collision detection
if (checkCollision(player, enemy)) {
    player.takeDamage(enemy.getAttackDamage());
}
```

Health and Damage:

- Define health and damage mechanics for players and enemies.
- Implement health management and damage calculation algorithms.

```cpp
// Example C++ code for health and damage mechanics
class Character {
private:
    int health;
public:
    void takeDamage(int damage) {
        health -= damage;
        if (health <= 0) {
            die();
        }
    }
};
```

Scoring and Points:

- Implement scoring and points mechanics to track player progress and achievements.
- Define conditions for earning points, such as defeating enemies, completing objectives, or collecting items.

```cpp
// Example C++ code for scoring and points
int playerScore = 0;

void enemyDefeated() {
    playerScore += 100; // Increment score when an enemy is
    defeated
}
```

Game States and Transitions:

- Define game states such as main menu, gameplay, pause menu, game over, etc.
- Implement state management to handle transitions between different game states.

```cpp
// Example C++ code for game states and transitions
enum GameState { MENU, PLAYING, PAUSED, GAME_OVER };
GameState currentState = MENU;

void updateGameState() {
    if (isGamePaused()) {
        currentState = PAUSED;
    }
    // Similar logic for other game state transitions
}
```

Power-Ups and Abilities:

- Define power-ups and special abilities that enhance player capabilities.
- Implement activation and usage mechanics for power-ups and abilities.

```cpp
// Example C++ code for power-ups and abilities
class Player {
public:
    void activatePowerUp(PowerUpType type) {
        if (type == DOUBLE_DAMAGE) {
            enableDoubleDamage();
        }
        // Similar implementations for other power-ups
    }
};
```

Game Rules and Logic:

- Define rules and logic that govern gameplay mechanics, interactions, and outcomes.
- Implement game rule checks and enforce rule-based behaviors.

```cpp
// Example C++ code for game rules and logic
bool isGameOver() {
    return player.isDead() || isTimeUp();
}
```

By implementing these game mechanics and rules in C++, developers can create interactive and engaging gameplay experiences that captivate players and keep them immersed in the game world.

Prototyping Your Game Ideas

One method for developing a clear idea of the game you want to make early on in the process with the least amount of time and work required is video game prototyping. With so many variables, influencers, and moving pieces, it's critical to be able to change course or refine your original plans if they prove to be unworkable.

Common video game prototyping techniques

We'll be examining various prototype methods in accordance with fidelity and complexity levels to maintain order.

Paper prototyping

Reducing your game to a simple paper prototype for a tabletop may initially seem almost unfeasible. At this point, the challenge is to distill the essence of your game into the smallest possible model that users can interact with.

Paper prototyping has the advantage of being the easiest and least expensive kind of prototype to set up. Paper prototypes for video games can be nothing more than rough drawings depicting the dimensions, placement, characteristics, and movements of the game's pieces.

Paper prototyping should be used to address certain key questions regarding your game, such as:

- Which way is the game world oriented? Take 2D or 3D environments, for instance.
- Which way are the characters and camera facing? For instance, first-person, top-down, etc.
- What dimensions of the world may the character move in?
- How will your system of inventory look like? Like, a grid or a list of items?
- Which menu systems do you want to utilize?

Wireframe prototyping

You should just be able to see the general direction the project is taking if you slightly squint your eyes. But a wireframe isn't the same as an artwork. It's a low-fidelity prototype designed to help players grasp game mechanics or layouts.

Character or environment model placement and relationships can be accurately depicted in a video game wireframe. More accuracy can also be achieved in the layout of in-game menus, loading screens, and other largely static experiences (such dialogue or Pokémon-esque battles). At this point, though, these depictions ought to be liberated from the limitations of art.

Gauging scale and location might be aided by using a surface that resembles a grid.

You can begin defining your game by using wireframes in the following ways:

- The characters that can be played or not (e.g., sorts of characters)
- The user interface or HUD (e.g., ability and health bars)
- A few of the game's set pieces or mechanisms (such dialogues)

Including artwork now would need an excessive amount of time and work. It may also lead you down a path from which it will be more expensive to turn back.

For instance, wireframe prototypes ought to be rather easy to make with Google Slides or PowerPoint. But with the help of apps like UXpin, designers can work together in real time and produce wireframes much more quickly. Depending on what you click, each static page may have buttons that lead to pre-selected other static pages.

Greybox prototyping

The process of greybox prototyping can be as easy as swapping out the 2D models for similarly generic 3D ones. But even in 2D games, there's a difference: a greybox prototype will have some of the physics from the finished product.

In racing games of the Burnout genre, this may simply mean grey cubes colliding with one another. Still, you may have included parts of the final collision, driving, and damage/health components already. Greybox prototypes are supposed to demonstrate the feel of a game, whereas wireframes and mockups are meant to show you how it will look. You can also begin constructing the real fonts or tracks, which will provide as the foundation for making distinct levels.

Once more, completed artwork shouldn't impede the development of greybox prototypes. For 3D models, even quite basic texturing and style can take a lot of time and effort.

Greybox prototype has the advantage of allowing you to begin using the final tools you'll need to construct your game. For instance, you could import physics blueprints and use Unreal Engine with basic, geometric static mesh models.

As you may guess, accurately scripting dynamic actions with paper mockups or wireframes is next to impossible. Greybox prototyping is also essential because it will enable you to evaluate many of the preliminary concepts for your mechanics and examine whether these interactions are functional. The increasing complexity of incorporating physics into the mix may cause many of the things you do to not go as planned.

Rapid prototyping

Rapid prototyping is a design process that relies on producing inexpensive, rapidly-evolving prototypes that get more complex. Although it's not exactly a novel concept, it's frequently seen as an enjoyable and thrilling technique to swiftly create lucrative and interesting games. World of Goo is a well-known instance.

The procedure entails quickly moving from a low-quality prototype to one with a little bit more fidelity. You repeat your ideas as many times as necessary, gradually improving them in tiny steps. Compared to brainstorming, video game prototyping is a more natural and hands-on method of game development. Plus, it's amazing to watch how a simple concept can evolve into a challenging and engaging game.

Getting Started with C++ Game Programming

Getting started with C++ game programming entails setting up your development environment, mastering the fundamentals of game development, and initiating the prototyping process. Initially, configuring your environment involves selecting a C++ compiler and an IDE, as well as integrating graphics libraries like OpenGL or DirectX for rendering graphics.

Once set up, delving into the fundamentals of game development entails grasping essential concepts such as player movement, collision detection, and game mechanics like health systems and scoring. Understanding principles of game design, such as clear objectives and meaningful choices, lays the groundwork for crafting engaging gameplay experiences.

Finally, prototyping your game ideas involves defining your concept, creating basic assets, and building a prototype to test and iterate upon, enabling you to refine your ideas and set the stage for full-scale development. Through this process, you'll embark on a rewarding journey to bring your game ideas to life using C++ game programming.

Understanding C++ Basics

The basics of C++ involves learning about variables, data types, control structures, functions, and classes. Let's explore each of these concepts with code examples and explanations:

Variables and Data Types:

- Variables are containers for storing data, and data types specify the type of data that a variable can hold.

```cpp
// Example of variable declaration and initialization
int score = 100;
float pi = 3.14;
char grade = 'A';
bool isGameOver = false;
```

Control Structures:

- Control structures allow you to control the flow of execution in a program, including conditional statements and loops.

```cpp
// Example of conditional statement (if-else)
if (score >= 90) {
    grade = 'A';
} else if (score >= 80) {
    grade = 'B';
} else {
    grade = 'C';
}

// Example of loop (for loop)
for (int i = 0; i < 5; i++) {
```

```cpp
    cout << "Iteration " << i << endl;
}
```

Functions:

- Functions are blocks of code that perform a specific task, and they can be called from other parts of the program.

```cpp
// Example of function declaration and definition
int add(int a, int b) {
    return a + b;
}

// Example of function call
int result = add(5, 3);
cout << "Result: " << result << endl;
```

Classes and Objects:

- Classes are user-defined data types that encapsulate data and functions into a single unit, and objects are instances of classes.

```cpp
// Example of class declaration
class Player {
public:
    string name;
    int health;

    void takeDamage(int damage) {
        health -= damage;
    }
};
```

```
// Example of object instantiation
Player player1;
player1.name = "Player 1";
player1.health = 100;
player1.takeDamage(20);
```

Understanding these basic concepts of C++ lays the foundation for writing more complex and functional programs. By mastering variables, control structures, functions, and classes, you'll be equipped to develop robust and efficient C++ applications and games.

Introduction to Object-Oriented Programming

Object-Oriented Programming (OOP) is a programming paradigm that revolves around the concept of objects, which are instances of classes. In OOP, objects encapsulate data (attributes) and behavior (methods) into a single unit, allowing for a more modular and organized approach to software development. OOP is based on several core principles, including:

- **Encapsulation**: Encapsulation involves bundling data and methods that operate on that data within a single unit (class). It hides the internal state of an object and only exposes the necessary interfaces for interacting with it. Encapsulation promotes data integrity and protects against unauthorized access or modification.
- **Inheritance**: Inheritance is a mechanism where a new class (subclass or derived class) inherits properties and behaviors from an existing class (superclass or base class). It allows for code reuse and the creation of a hierarchy of classes, where subclasses can specialize or extend the functionality of their superclass.
- **Polymorphism**: Polymorphism allows objects of different classes to be treated as objects of a common superclass. It enables dynamic binding and method overriding, where a method in a subclass can override a

method with the same name in its superclass. Polymorphism promotes flexibility and extensibility by allowing code to be written in a more generic and reusable manner.

- **Abstraction**: Abstraction involves simplifying complex systems by focusing on the essential characteristics and hiding unnecessary details. In OOP, abstraction is achieved through classes and interfaces, which define a blueprint for creating objects without specifying their internal implementation. Abstraction promotes modularity and separation of concerns by allowing developers to work with high-level concepts rather than low-level details.

OOP facilitates modular, maintainable, and scalable software development by organizing code into reusable and self-contained units (objects). By leveraging encapsulation, inheritance, polymorphism, and abstraction, developers can design more robust, flexible, and understandable code structures that are easier to manage, extend, and maintain over time.

Object-Oriented Programming (OOP) is widely used in C++ game development due to its ability to organize code into reusable and modular components, making it easier to manage complex game systems. Let's explore how OOP principles are applied in C++ game development with code examples and explanations:

Classes and Objects:

- **Classes**: In C++ game development, classes are used to define the blueprint for game entities such as players, enemies, items, and levels. Each class encapsulates data (attributes) and behavior (methods) related to a specific game entity.

```cpp
// Example of a Player class
class Player {
private:
    int health;
    int score;

public:
    void takeDamage(int damage) {
        health -= damage;
    }

    void increaseScore(int points) {
        score += points;
    }
};
```

- **Objects**: Objects of these classes represent specific instances of game entities with their own unique properties and behaviors.

```cpp
// Example of creating objects from the Player class
Player player1;
Player player2;

player1.takeDamage(10);
player2.increaseScore(100);
```

Inheritance:

- **Inheritance**: In C++ game development, inheritance is used to create class hierarchies where subclasses inherit properties and behaviors from a superclass. This allows for code reuse and the creation of specialized game entities.

```cpp
// Example of inheritance
class Enemy : public Entity {
private:
    int damage;

public:
    void attack(Player& target) {
        target.takeDamage(damage);
    }
};
```

Polymorphism:

- **Polymorphism**: Polymorphism in C++ game development allows for the use of objects of different classes through a common interface. This enables dynamic binding and method overriding, facilitating flexibility and extensibility.

```cpp
// Example of polymorphism
void applyPowerUp(Player& player, PowerUp& powerUp) {
    powerUp.applyEffect(player);
}
```

Encapsulation:

- **Encapsulation**: Encapsulation in C++ game development involves hiding the internal implementation details of game entities and providing well-defined interfaces for interacting with them. This promotes data integrity and helps prevent unintended modification.

```cpp
// Example of encapsulation
class PowerUp {
```

```
public:
    virtual void applyEffect(Player& player) = 0;
};
```

By leveraging OOP principles such as classes, objects, inheritance, polymorphism, and encapsulation, C++ game developers can create well-structured and maintainable codebases that facilitate the development of complex and scalable games. OOP enables developers to design modular components, reuse code effectively, and manage game entities and systems with ease, resulting in more efficient and robust game development workflows. These concepts will be used later in real game scenarios in this book.

Working with Data Structures in C++ and Algorithms

Data structures and algorithms (DSA) are fundamental building blocks for efficient C++ game development. They determine how you organize and manipulate game data, ultimately impacting the performance and smoothness of your game.

Here's a breakdown of why DSA is important for C++ game development:

- **Efficient Data Management:** Games deal with a lot of data – enemy positions, player inventory, level maps, etc. Choosing the right data structure allows you to store, access, and update this data quickly, leading to a more responsive game.
- **Game Mechanics:** Many core mechanics rely on DSA. Collision detection between characters and objects uses spatial data structures like quadtrees or octrees. Pathfinding for AI-controlled enemies often involves algorithms like A*.
- **Performance Optimization:** A well-written game should run smoothly. By understanding how different algorithms perform, you can optimize your code to ensure the game runs at a steady frame rate.

Let's explore how common data structures and algorithms are used in C++ game development.

Data Structures:

Arrays: Arrays are used to store a fixed-size collection of elements, commonly used for storing grid-based game data like tile maps.

```cpp
// Example of an array for storing tile map data
const int MAP_WIDTH = 10;
const int MAP_HEIGHT = 10;
int tileMap[MAP_WIDTH][MAP_HEIGHT];
```

Vectors: Vectors provide dynamic resizing and efficient element access, suitable for managing lists of game objects or entities.

```cpp
// Example of a vector for storing game objects
#include <vector>
std::vector<GameObject> gameObjects;
```

Linked Lists:

Linked Lists: Linked lists are useful for dynamic data structures where elements can be easily inserted, removed, or rearranged, such as managing spawn queues for enemies.

```cpp
// Example of a linked list node for managing spawn queues
struct EnemyNode {
    Enemy enemy;
    EnemyNode* next;
};
```

Maps and Sets:

Maps: Maps are used for fast retrieval of data, such as storing game entities with unique identifiers.

```cpp
// Example of a map for storing game entities
#include <map>
std::map<int, Entity> entityMap;
```

Sets: Sets are useful for managing collections of unique elements, such as tracking active power-ups.

```cpp
// Example of a set for tracking active power-ups
#include <set>
std::set<PowerUp> activePowerUps;
```

Algorithms:

Sorting Algorithms:

Sorting algorithms are essential for organizing game data efficiently, such as sorting entities by their position for rendering.

```cpp
// Example of sorting entities by their position using std::sort
std::sort(entities.begin(), entities.end(), [](const Entity& a,
const Entity& b) {
    return a.position < b.position;
});
```

Pathfinding Algorithms:

Pathfinding algorithms are used for finding optimal paths for game entities, such as A* for navigating through a game world.

```
// Example of A* pathfinding algorithm for navigating through a
tile-based map
std::vector<Tile> findPath(Tile start, Tile goal) {
    // Implementation of A* algorithm
}
```

Collision Detection Algorithms:

Collision detection algorithms are crucial for detecting collisions between game objects, such as AABB collision detection for 2D games.

```
// Example of AABB collision detection algorithm for 2D game
objects
bool checkCollision(const GameObject& obj1, const GameObject&
obj2) {
    // Implementation of AABB collision detection
}
```

By leveraging these data structures and algorithms effectively, C++ game developers can optimize performance, manage game state efficiently, and implement complex gameplay mechanics with ease. Choosing the right data structure and algorithm for the specific requirements of the game is essential for achieving optimal performance and scalability.

II

Advanced Topics and Project Development

Advanced Topics in C++ Game Development

Shader Programming with GLSL

Shader programming with GLSL (OpenGL Shading Language) unlocks a powerful tool for creating stunning visuals in your 3D applications and games. Here's a breakdown of what it is and how it works:

What is GLSL?

GLSL is a C-like programming language specifically designed to work with the graphics pipeline in OpenGL (or WebGL for web graphics). Shaders are small programs written in GLSL that are uploaded to the GPU (Graphics Processing Unit). The GPU then executes these programs on a vertex-by-vertex or pixel-by-pixel basis, allowing you to precisely control how objects are rendered on the screen.

Types of Shaders:

There are various types of shaders, but two primary ones handle most of the 3D rendering tasks:

Vertex Shaders

These shaders manipulate the positions of vertices in 3D space. They can be used for tasks like transforming objects, applying lighting calculations, or skinning animations for characters.

A simple Vertex Shader

```
// Example of a simple vertex shader
#version 330 core
layout (location = 0) in vec3 aPosition;
layout (location = 1) in vec3 aColor;
out vec3 vColor;
void main() {
gl_Position = vec4(aPosition, 1.0);
vColor = aColor; }
```

Fragment Shaders:

These shaders determine the final color of each pixel on the screen. They receive information from the vertex shader and use it to calculate lighting, apply textures, or create special effects like shadows or reflections.

```
// Example of a simple fragment shader
#version 330 core
in vec3 vColor;
out vec4 FragColor;
void main() {
FragColor = vec4(vColor, 1.0);
}
```

How Shaders Work:

Vertex Data: 3D objects are defined by vertices (points in space) and their attributes (color, texture coordinates, etc.). This data is sent to the GPU.

Vertex Shader: The vertex shader is executed for each vertex. It processes the vertex data, including transformations, lighting calculations, and potentially modifying attributes.

Clipping: After processing, vertices are clipped to the viewing frustum (the visible area of the scene) and converted into clip space coordinates.

Rasterization: Clipped vertices are converted into fragments (pixels on the screen).

Fragment Shader: The fragment shader is executed for each fragment. It receives data from the vertex shader (like interpolated vertex attributes) and calculates the final color of the fragment based on lighting, textures, and other effects.

Fragment Processing: The calculated fragment colors are blended and written to the frame buffer, resulting in the final image you see on the screen.

Let's consider a simple 2D game using OpenGL and shaders. In this example, we'll create a basic game where a player controls a character that moves around and collects coins. We'll use shaders for rendering the game objects and applying simple effects like color changes.

Setting Up the Environment:

First, we need to set up our development environment. We'll use GLFW for window management and GLEW for OpenGL extension loading. Additionally, we'll need a simple shader program to render our game objects.

```cpp
#include <iostream>
#include <GL/glew.h>
#include <GLFW/glfw3.h>

const char* vertexShaderSource = R"(
```

```cpp
    #version 330 core
    layout (location = 0) in vec2 position;

    void main() {
        gl_Position = vec4(position.x, position.y, 0.0, 1.0);
    }
)";

const char* fragmentShaderSource = R"(
    #version 330 core
    out vec4 FragColor;

    void main() {
        FragColor = vec4(1.0, 0.0, 0.0, 1.0); // Red color
    }
)";

int main() {
    // Initialize GLFW
    glfwInit();
    glfwWindowHint(GLFW_CONTEXT_VERSION_MAJOR, 3);
    glfwWindowHint(GLFW_CONTEXT_VERSION_MINOR, 3);
    glfwWindowHint(GLFW_OPENGL_PROFILE, GLFW_OPENGL_CORE_PROFILE);

    // Create a GLFW window
    GLFWwindow* window = glfwCreateWindow(800, 600, "Simple
    Game", NULL, NULL);
    if (window == NULL) {
        std::cout << "Failed to create GLFW window" << std::endl;
        glfwTerminate();
        return -1;
    }
    glfwMakeContextCurrent(window);

    // Initialize GLEW
    glewExperimental = true;
    if (glewInit() != GLEW_OK) {
        std::cout << "Failed to initialize GLEW" << std::endl;
        return -1;
    }
```

```cpp
    // Create and compile shaders
    unsigned int vertexShader = glCreateShader(GL_VERTEX_SHADER);
    glShaderSource(vertexShader, 1, &vertexShaderSource, NULL);
    glCompileShader(vertexShader);

    unsigned int fragmentShader =
    glCreateShader(GL_FRAGMENT_SHADER);
    glShaderSource(fragmentShader, 1, &fragmentShaderSource,
    NULL);
    glCompileShader(fragmentShader);

    // Create shader program
    unsigned int shaderProgram = glCreateProgram();
    glAttachShader(shaderProgram, vertexShader);
    glAttachShader(shaderProgram, fragmentShader);
    glLinkProgram(shaderProgram);

    // Main game loop
    while (!glfwWindowShouldClooc(window)) {
        // Input handling
        // ...

        // Rendering
        glClear(GL_COLOR_BUFFER_BIT);
        glUseProgram(shaderProgram);
        // Draw game objects
        // ...

        // Swap buffers
        glfwSwapBuffers(window);
        glfwPollEvents();
    }

    // Clean up
    glfwTerminate();
    return 0;
}
```

Rendering Game Objects:

In the main game loop, we'll render our game objects using the shader program we created. We'll define vertices for our game objects (e.g., player character, coins) and render them using OpenGL.

```cpp
// Vertices for a simple square representing the player character
float vertices[] = {
    -0.5f, -0.5f, // bottom-left corner
     0.5f, -0.5f,  // bottom-right corner
     0.5f,  0.5f,  // top-right corner
     0.5f,  0.5f,  // top-right corner
    -0.5f, 0.5f,   // top-left corner
    -0.5f, -0.5f  // bottom-left corner
};

// Vertex buffer object (VBO) and vertex array object (VAO) setup
unsigned int VBO, VAO;
glGenVertexArrays(1, &VAO);
glGenBuffers(1, &VBO);
glBindVertexArray(VAO);
glBindBuffer(GL_ARRAY_BUFFER, VBO);
glBufferData(GL_ARRAY_BUFFER, sizeof(vertices), vertices,
GL_STATIC_DRAW);
glVertexAttribPointer(0, 2, GL_FLOAT, GL_FALSE, 2 *
sizeof(float), (void*)0);
glEnableVertexAttribArray(0);
glBindBuffer(GL_ARRAY_BUFFER, 0);
glBindVertexArray(0);

// Rendering loop
while (!glfwWindowShouldClose(window)) {
    // Input handling
    // ...
    // Rendering
    glClear(GL_COLOR_BUFFER_BIT);
    glUseProgram(shaderProgram);
    glBindVertexArray(VAO);
    glDrawArrays(GL_TRIANGLES, 0, 6);

    // Swap buffers
```

```
    glfwSwapBuffers(window);
    glfwPollEvents();
}
```

Shader Effects:

We can apply simple shader effects by modifying the fragment shader. For example, let's add a uniform variable to control the color of the player character:

```
#version 330 core
out vec4 FragColor;

uniform vec3 objectColor; // Color uniform

void main() {
    FragColor = vec4(objectColor, 1.0);
}
```

Then, we can set the color uniform value in C++ and pass it to the shader:

```
// Get uniform location
int objectColorLocation = glGetUniformLocation(shaderProgram,
"objectColor");

// Set uniform value
glUniform3f(objectColorLocation, 1.0f, 0.5f, 0.2f); // Orange
color
```

In this example, we've created a simple 2D game using C++ and OpenGL shaders. We rendered game objects using a shader program and applied a simple color effect using shader uniforms. This demonstrates the basics of using shaders in C++ game development to achieve graphical effects and render game scenes.

Advanced Graphics Techniques

Advanced graphics techniques in C++ involve leveraging modern rendering APIs like OpenGL or Vulkan to achieve stunning visual effects and realistic graphics in games and applications. Let's explore some of these techniques along with code examples where applicable:

Deferred Rendering:

Deferred rendering is a technique that separates the rendering process into two stages: geometry rendering and lighting. It allows for more complex lighting effects and reduces the number of shader invocations per frame.

```cpp
// Deferred vertex shader
const char* deferredVertexShaderSource = R"(
    #version 330 core
    layout (location = 0) in vec3 aPos;
    layout (location = 1) in vec3 aNormal;
    layout (location = 2) in vec2 aTexCoords;

    out vec3 FragPos;
    out vec3 Normal;
    out vec2 TexCoords;

    uniform mat4 model;
    uniform mat4 view;
    uniform mat4 projection;

    void main() {
        FragPos = vec3(model * vec4(aPos, 1.0));
        Normal = mat3(transpose(inverse(model))) * aNormal;
        TexCoords = aTexCoords;
        gl_Position = projection * view * vec4(FragPos, 1.0);
    }
)";

// Deferred fragment shader (geometry pass)
```

```cpp
const char* deferredGeometryFragmentShaderSource = R"(
    #version 330 core
    layout (location = 0) out vec3 gPosition;
    layout (location = 1) out vec3 gNormal;
    layout (location = 2) out vec3 gAlbedoSpec;

    in vec3 FragPos;
    in vec3 Normal;
    in vec2 TexCoords;

    uniform sampler2D textureDiffuse;
    uniform sampler2D textureNormal;
    uniform sampler2D textureSpecular;

    void main() {
        gPosition = FragPos;
        gNormal = normalize(Normal);
        gAlbedoSpec = texture(textureDiffuse, TexCoords).rgb;
        gAlbedoSpec.a = texture(textureSpecular, TexCoords).r; //
        Store specular intensity in alpha channel
    }
)";

// Deferred fragment shader (lighting pass)
const char* deferredLightingFragmentShaderSource = R"(
    #version 330 core
    out vec4 FragColor;

    in vec2 TexCoords;

    uniform sampler2D gPosition;
    uniform sampler2D gNormal;
    uniform sampler2D gAlbedoSpec;

    struct Light {
        vec3 position;
        vec3 color;
        float intensity;
    };
```

```cpp
uniform Light lights[MAX_LIGHTS]; // Array of lights
uniform int numLights; // Number of lights

void main() {
    vec3 FragPos = texture(gPosition, TexCoords).rgb;
    vec3 Normal = texture(gNormal, TexCoords).rgb;
    vec3 Albedo = texture(gAlbedoSpec, TexCoords).rgb;
    float Specular = texture(gAlbedoSpec, TexCoords).a;

    // Lighting calculations
    vec3 lighting = vec3(0.0);
    for (int i = 0; i < numLights; ++i) {
        // Calculate lighting contribution from each light
        // ...
    }

    FragColor = vec4(lighting * Albedo + Specular, 1.0);
}
)";

// Main rendering loop
while (!glfwWindowShouldClose(window)) {
    // Input handling
    // ...

    // Geometry pass: render scene geometry to G-buffer
    glBindFramebuffer(GL_FRAMEBUFFER, gBuffer);
    glClear(GL_COLOR_BUFFER_BIT | GL_DEPTH_BUFFER_BIT);
    glUseProgram(deferredGeometryShaderProgram);
    renderSceneGeometry(); // Render scene geometry using
deferred geometry shader

    // Lighting pass: render lights using G-buffer textures
    glBindFramebuffer(GL_FRAMEBUFFER, 0);
    glClear(GL_COLOR_BUFFER_BIT);
    glUseProgram(deferredLightingShaderProgram);
    bindGBufferTextures(); // Bind G-buffer textures
    renderLights(); // Render lights using deferred lighting
shader
```

```
    // Swap buffers
    glfwSwapBuffers(window);
    glfwPollEvents();
}
```

In this example:

- We have two fragment shaders: one for the geometry pass and one for the lighting pass in deferred rendering.
- In the geometry pass (**deferredGeometryFragmentShaderSource**), we render scene geometry to multiple render targets (G-buffer) to store position, normal, albedo, and specular information.
- In the lighting pass (**deferredLightingFragmentShaderSource**), we calculate lighting contributions from multiple lights using the information stored in the G-buffer.
- In the main rendering loop, we switch between the geometry pass and the lighting pass by binding different framebuffers. We render scene geometry in the geometry pass and render lights in the lighting pass.

Please note that this is a simplified example. In a real-world application, you would need to handle additional optimizations, such as deferred shading, deferred lighting, and handle multiple render targets efficiently.

Physically Based Rendering (PBR):

PBR is a rendering technique that simulates the interaction of light with materials in a physically accurate manner. It relies on shaders and material properties to achieve realistic lighting and shading effects.

```
// PBR vertex shader
const char* pbrVertexShaderSource = R"(
    #version 330 core
```

```glsl
    layout (location = 0) in vec3 aPos;
    layout (location = 1) in vec3 aNormal;
    layout (location = 2) in vec2 aTexCoords;

    out vec3 FragPos;
    out vec3 Normal;
    out vec2 TexCoords;

    uniform mat4 model;
    uniform mat4 view;
    uniform mat4 projection;

    void main() {
        FragPos = vec3(model * vec4(aPos, 1.0));
        Normal = mat3(transpose(inverse(model))) * aNormal;
        TexCoords = aTexCoords;
        gl_Position = projection * view * vec4(FragPos, 1.0);
    }
)";

// PBR fragment shader
const char* pbrFragmentShaderSource = R"(
    #version 330 core
    out vec4 FragColor;

    in vec3 FragPos;
    in vec3 Normal;
    in vec2 TexCoords;

    uniform vec3 albedo;
    uniform float metallic;
    uniform float roughness;
    uniform float ao;

    // Function to calculate Fresnel term (Schlick's
    approximation)
    float fresnelSchlick(float cosTheta, vec3 F0) {
        return pow(1.0 - cosTheta, 5.0) + F0 * (1.0 - pow(1.0 -
        cosTheta, 5.0));
    }
```

```cpp
    void main() {
        vec3 N = normalize(Normal);
        vec3 V = normalize(-FragPos); // View direction
        vec3 R = reflect(-V, N); // Reflection direction

        vec3 F0 = vec3(0.04); // Default specular reflection
        (dielectric)
        vec3 Lo = vec3(0.0); // Outgoing light

        // Calculate lighting contributions
        // ...

        // Calculate Fresnel term
        float cosTheta = max(dot(N, V), 0.0);
        vec3 F = fresnelSchlick(cosTheta, F0);

        // Calculate specular reflection
        vec3 specular = F * Lo;

        // Final color = (albedo * diffuse) + specular
        vec3 color = albedo * (Lo + specular);

        FragColor = vec4(color, 1.0);
    }
)";

// Main rendering loop
while (!glfwWindowShouldClose(window)) {
    // Input handling
    // ...

    // Rendering
    glClear(GL_COLOR_BUFFER_BIT | GL_DEPTH_BUFFER_BIT);
    glUseProgram(pbrShaderProgram);
    // Set shader uniforms
    // Bind textures
    renderScene(); // Render scene using PBR shader

    // Swap buffers
```

```
    glfwSwapBuffers(window);
    glfwPollEvents();
}
```

In this example:

- The vertex shader (**pbrVertexShaderSource**) calculates the position, normal, and texture coordinates of each vertex in world space. It transforms these values to screen space and passes them to the fragment shader.
- The fragment shader (**pbrFragmentShaderSource**) calculates the PBR lighting equation to determine the final color of each pixel. It takes into account the material's albedo, metallicness, roughness, ambient occlusion, and Fresnel term for specular reflection.
- The **fresnelSchlick** function calculates the Fresnel term using Schlick's approximation.
- In the main rendering loop, we use the PBR shader program to render the scene. We set shader uniforms for material properties and bind textures (albedo, metallic, roughness, etc.) before rendering the scene.

Please note that this is a simplified example. In a real-world application, you would need to handle texture sampling, lighting calculations (diffuse, specular, ambient), and other optimizations to achieve realistic PBR rendering.

Shadow Mapping:

Shadow mapping is a technique used to simulate shadows in a scene by rendering depth maps from the perspective of a light source and comparing them to the depth of objects from the camera's perspective.

```
// Shadow vertex shader
const char* shadowVertexShaderSource = R"(
```

```cpp
    #version 330 core
    layout (location = 0) in vec3 aPos;

    uniform mat4 lightSpaceMatrix;
    uniform mat4 model;

    void main() {
        gl_Position = lightSpaceMatrix * model * vec4(aPos, 1.0);
    }
)";

// Shadow fragment shader (empty, no need for fragment shader in
shadow pass)
const char* shadowFragmentShaderSource = R"(
    #version 330 core
    void main() {}
)";

// Main rendering loop
while (!glfwWindowShouldClose(window)) {
    // Input handling
    // ...

    // Shadow pass: render scene from light's perspective to
    depth map
    glUseProgram(shadowShaderProgram);
    glBindFramebuffer(GL_FRAMEBUFFER, depthMapFBO);
    glClear(GL_DEPTH_BUFFER_BIT);
    renderSceneFromLight(); // Render scene from light's
    perspective

    // Reset framebuffer
    glBindFramebuffer(GL_FRAMEBUFFER, 0);

    // Main pass: render scene from camera's perspective
    glUseProgram(shaderProgram);
    glClear(GL_COLOR_BUFFER_BIT | GL_DEPTH_BUFFER_BIT);
    // Set shader uniforms and textures
    glUniformMatrix4fv(lightSpaceMatrixLocation, 1, GL_FALSE,
    &lightSpaceMatrix[0][0]);
```

```cpp
glBindTexture(GL_TEXTURE_2D, depthMapTexture);
renderSceneFromCamera(); // Render scene from camera's
perspective

// Swap buffers
glfwSwapBuffers(window);
glfwPollEvents();
}
```

In this example, we have two shader programs: one for the shadow pass (**shadowVertexShaderSource**) and one for the main rendering pass. During the shadow pass, we render the scene from the perspective of the light source to generate a depth map (shadow map). We then use this depth map in the main rendering pass to calculate shadows. **lightSpaceMatrix** transforms vertices from world space to light space.

The **renderSceneFromLight()** and **renderSceneFromCamera()** functions are placeholders for rendering the scene from the light's perspective and the camera's perspective, respectively. These functions would involve setting up vertex buffers, binding textures, and drawing objects using appropriate shaders.

Please note that this is a simplified example. In a real-world application, you would need to handle shadow map resolution, filtering, biasing, and other optimizations to improve shadow quality and reduce artifacts.

Screen-Space Reflections (SSR):

SSR is a technique used to simulate reflections by ray tracing in screen space. It allows for realistic reflections of objects and environments without the need for complex geometry.

```cpp
// Vertex shader
const char* vertexShaderSource = R"(
    #version 330 core
    layout (location = 0) in vec3 aPos;
    layout (location = 1) in vec2 aTexCoords;

    out vec2 TexCoords;

    void main() {
        gl_Position = vec4(aPos, 1.0);
        TexCoords = aTexCoords;
    }
)";

// Fragment shader
const char* fragmentShaderSource = R"(
    #version 330 core
    in vec2 TexCoords;
    out vec4 FragColor;

    uniform sampler2D textureColor;
    uniform sampler2D textureNormal;

    const float stepSize = 0.01; // SSR step size

    void main() {
        vec3 viewDir = normalize(texture(textureNormal,
        TexCoords).xyz); // View direction
        vec3 reflectDir = reflect(viewDir, vec3(0.0, 0.0, 1.0));
        // Reflected direction

        // SSR ray marching
        float depth = 1.0; // Starting depth
        float visibility = 1.0; // Initial visibility
        for (int i = 0; i < 50; ++i) { // Max iterations
            vec2 texCoords = TexCoords - reflectDir.xy * depth;
            // Calculate texture coordinates along reflection ray
            float sampledDepth = texture(textureDepth,
            texCoords).r; // Sample depth texture
            visibility *= 1.0 - stepSize * (1.0 - sampledDepth);
```

```cpp
        // Accumulate visibility
        depth += stepSize; // Increment depth
    }

    FragColor = texture(textureColor, TexCoords) *
    visibility; // Apply visibility to color
  }
)";

// Main rendering loop
while (!glfwWindowShouldClose(window)) {
    // Input handling
    // ...

    // Rendering
    glClear(GL_COLOR_BUFFER_BIT | GL_DEPTH_BUFFER_BIT);
    glUseProgram(shaderProgram);
    // Bind textures (color, normal, depth)
    // Set uniforms
    // Render scene
    // ...

    // Swap buffers
    glfwSwapBuffers(window);
    glfwPollEvents();
}
```

In this example, we calculate SSR by ray marching through the screen space using the reflected view direction. We sample the depth buffer to determine visibility along the reflection ray, accumulating visibility along the way. Finally, we apply the accumulated visibility to the color texture to produce the final SSR effect.

Please note that this is a simplified example, and implementing SSR in a production-level application may require additional optimizations and considerations, such as handling multiple reflection bounces and dealing with screen space artifacts.

Ambient Occlusion:

Ambient occlusion is a shading technique used to simulate the soft shadows that occur in areas where objects are close together, resulting in reduced ambient lighting.

```
// Ambient Occlusion fragment shader
const char* aoFragmentShaderSource = R"(
    #version 330 core
    out float FragColor;

    in vec2 TexCoords;

    uniform sampler2D depthMap;
    uniform sampler2D normalMap;
    uniform vec2 noiseScale; // Scale factor for noise texture
    uniform int kernelSize; // Number of samples in the AO kernel

    // Array of sample directions for AO
    const vec2 sampleDirections[16] = {
        vec2(-1.0, -1.0), vec2(0.0, -1.0), vec2(1.0, -1.0),
        vec2(-1.0,  0.0), vec2(0.0,  0.0), vec2(1.0,  0.0),
        vec2(-1.0,  1.0), vec2(0.0,  1.0), vec2(1.0,  1.0),
        vec2(-1.0, -1.0), vec2(0.0, -1.0), vec2(1.0, -1.0),
        vec2(-1.0,  0.0), vec2(0.0,  0.0), vec2(1.0,  0.0),
        vec2(-1.0,  1.0), vec2(0.0,  1.0), vec2(1.0,  1.0)
    };

    void main() {
        // Sample depth and normal from textures
        float centerDepth = texture(depthMap, TexCoords).r;
        vec3 centerNormal = normalize(texture(normalMap,
        TexCoords).rgb);

        // AO calculation using sample directions
        float ao = 0.0;
        for (int i = 0; i < kernelSize; ++i) {
            vec2 sampleCoord = TexCoords + noiseScale *
            sampleDirections[i];
```

```cpp
        float sampleDepth = texture(depthMap, sampleCoord).r;
        vec3 sampleNormal = normalize(texture(normalMap,
        sampleCoord).rgb);

        float depthDifference = centerDepth - sampleDepth;
        float distance = length(noiseScale *
        sampleDirections[i]);
        float occlusionFactor = max(0.0, 1.0 -
        depthDifference / distance);
        float normalDifference = dot(centerNormal,
        sampleNormal);
        ao += occlusionFactor * normalDifference;
    }

    // Final AO calculation
    ao /= float(kernelSize);
    FragColor = 1.0 - ao; // Invert AO for better
    visualization
  }
)";

// Main rendering loop
while (!glfwWindowShouldClose(window)) {
    // Input handling
    // ...

    // Rendering
    glClear(GL_COLOR_BUFFER_BIT | GL_DEPTH_BUFFER_BIT);
    glUseProgram(aoShaderProgram);
    // Set shader uniforms
    renderScene(); // Render scene using AO shader

    // Swap buffers
    glfwSwapBuffers(window);
    glfwPollEvents();
}
```

In this example:

- We calculate Ambient Occlusion (AO) in the fragment shader by sampling

depths and normals from depth and normal maps.
- We define an array of sample directions (sampleDirections) to sample points around the current fragment for AO calculation.
- For each sample direction, we sample depth and normal from the textures and calculate occlusion factor based on depth difference and normal similarity.
- We accumulate occlusion factors from all samples and calculate the final AO value by averaging over the kernel size.

Finally, we invert the AO value for better visualization (optional).

Please note that this is a simplified example. In a real-world application, you would need to handle additional optimizations, such as bilateral filtering, to reduce noise and improve AO quality. Additionally, you may need to adjust parameters like kernel size and noise scale for better results.

Post-Processing Effects:

Post-processing effects are applied to the final rendered image to enhance or alter its appearance. Examples include bloom, depth of field, motion blur, and color grading.

```cpp
// Post-processing fragment shader (Bloom)
const char* bloomFragmentShaderSource = R"(
    #version 330 core
    out vec4 FragColor;

    in vec2 TexCoords;

    uniform sampler2D sceneTexture;
    uniform sampler2D bloomTexture;

    void main() {
        vec4 sceneColor = texture(sceneTexture, TexCoords);
        vec4 bloomColor = texture(bloomTexture, TexCoords);
```

```cpp
        FragColor = sceneColor + bloomColor; // Add bloom to
        scene color
    }
)";

// Post-processing fragment shader (Depth of Field)
const char* dofFragmentShaderSource = R"(
    #version 330 core
    out vec4 FragColor;

    in vec2 TexCoords;

    uniform sampler2D sceneTexture;
    uniform float focalDepth;
    uniform float focalLength;
    uniform float aperture;

    void main() {
        vec4 color = texture(sceneTexture, TexCoords);
        float depth = texture(sceneDepth, TexCoords).r;
        float focalDistance = abs(focalDepth - depth);
        float blurFactor = min(1.0, focalDistance / focalLength)
        * aperture;
        FragColor = applyBlur(TexCoords, color, blurFactor); //
        Apply blur based on focal distance
    }
)";

// Post-processing fragment shader (Motion Blur)
const char* motionBlurFragmentShaderSource = R"(
    #version 330 core
    out vec4 FragColor;

    in vec2 TexCoords;

    uniform sampler2D sceneTexture;
    uniform sampler2D velocityTexture;
    uniform float blurAmount;

    void main() {
```

```cpp
        vec4 color = vec4(0.0);
        vec2 velocity = texture(velocityTexture, TexCoords).xy *
        blurAmount;
        for (int i = -4; i <= 4; ++i) {
            vec2 offset = float(i) * velocity;
            color += texture(sceneTexture, TexCoords + offset);
        }
        FragColor = color / 9.0; // Average colors to get final
        result
    }
)";


// Post-processing fragment shader (Color Grading)
const char* colorGradingFragmentShaderSource = R"(
    #version 330 core
    out vec4 FragColor;

    in vec2 TexCoords;

    uniform sampler2D sceneTexture;
    uniform vec3 colorFilter;
    uniform float brightness;
    uniform float contrast;
    uniform float saturation;

    void main() {
        vec4 color = texture(sceneTexture, TexCoords);
        // Apply color grading operations (e.g., brightness,
        contrast, saturation)
        color.rgb = clamp(color.rgb * brightness, 0.0, 1.0); //
        Adjust brightness
        color.rgb = mix(vec3(0.5), color.rgb, contrast); //
        Adjust contrast
        float averageColor = dot(color.rgb, vec3(0.3333));
        color.rgb = mix(vec3(averageColor), color.rgb,
        saturation); // Adjust saturation
        color.rgb = clamp(color.rgb + colorFilter, 0.0, 1.0); //
        Apply color filter
        FragColor = color;
    }
```

```cpp
)";

// Main rendering loop
while (!glfwWindowShouldClose(window)) {
    // Input handling
    // ...

    // Rendering
    glClear(GL_COLOR_BUFFER_BIT | GL_DEPTH_BUFFER_BIT);
    renderScene(); // Render scene

    // Apply post-processing effects
    glBindFramebuffer(GL_FRAMEBUFFER, postProcessingFBO);
    glClear(GL_COLOR_BUFFER_BIT);
    glUseProgram(bloomShaderProgram);
    renderFullScreenQuad(); // Render full-screen quad for bloom
    glUseProgram(dofShaderProgram);
    renderFullScreenQuad(); // Render full-screen quad for depth
    of field
    glUseProgram(motionBlurShaderProgram);
    renderFullScreenQuad(); // Render full-screen quad for motion
    blur
    glUseProgram(colorGradingShaderProgram);
    renderFullScreenQuad(); // Render full-screen quad for color
    grading

    // Swap buffers
    glfwSwapBuffers(window);
    glfwPollEvents();
}
```

In this example:

- We have separate fragment shaders for each post-processing effect: bloom, depth of field (DOF), motion blur, and color grading.
- Each fragment shader takes the scene texture as input and applies the corresponding effect.
- In the main rendering loop, we render the scene and then apply the post-processing effects by rendering a full-screen quad with the corresponding

shader program.

- Each effect may have additional parameters (e.g., aperture for DOF, blur amount for motion blur) that can be adjusted to achieve desired results.

Note that this is a simplified example. In a real-world application, you may need to handle additional optimizations, such as down sampling for bloom, depth buffer sampling for DOF, velocity buffer generation for motion blur, and advanced color grading operations for better visual quality.

GPU Compute Shaders:

Compute shaders are used to offload complex computations to the GPU, allowing for parallel processing and acceleration of tasks such as physics simulations, particle systems, and procedural generation.

```cpp
// Compute shader source code
const char* computeShaderSource = R"(
    #version 430 core
    layout (local_size_x = 16, local_size_y = 16) in;

    uniform float factor;

    layout (binding = 0, rgba32f) uniform image2D inputImage;
    layout (binding = 1, rgba32f) uniform image2D outputImage;

    void main() {
        ivec2 pixelCoords = ivec2(gl_GlobalInvocationID.xy);
        vec4 inputColor = imageLoad(inputImage, pixelCoords);
        vec4 outputColor = inputColor * factor;
        imageStore(outputImage, pixelCoords, outputColor);
    }
)";

// Main rendering loop
while (!glfwWindowShouldClose(window)) {
    // Input handling
```

```cpp
// ...

    // Dispatch compute shader
    glUseProgram(computeShaderProgram);
    glBindImageTexture(0, inputTexture, 0, GL_FALSE, 0,
    GL_READ_ONLY, GL_RGBA32F);
    glBindImageTexture(1, outputTexture, 0, GL_FALSE, 0,
    GL_WRITE_ONLY, GL_RGBA32F);
    glUniform1f(factorLocation, computeFactor); // Set shader
    uniform
    glDispatchCompute(numGroupsX, numGroupsY, 1);

    // Wait for the compute shader to finish
    glMemoryBarrier(GL_SHADER_IMAGE_ACCESS_BARRIER_BIT);

    // Rendering
    // ...

    // Swap buffers
    glfwSwapBuffers(window);
    glfwPollEvents();
}
```

In this example:

- We define a compute shader (**computeShaderSource**) that takes an input image, processes it, and stores the result in an output image.
- The main rendering loop dispatches the compute shader using **glDispatchCompute**, specifying the number of work groups to execute.
- Before and after executing the compute shader, we use **glMemoryBarrier** to ensure proper synchronization between the CPU and GPU.
- Inside the compute shader, we use **imageLoad** and **imageStore** functions to read from and write to image textures.
- We bind input and output image textures using **glBindImageTexture**.
- We set shader uniforms (e.g., factor) using **glUniform1f**.

Please note that this is a simplified example. In a real-world application, you may need to handle more complex data processing tasks, coordinate systems, synchronization, and memory management for optimal performance and correctness.

By incorporating these advanced graphics techniques into C++ applications using modern rendering APIs like OpenGL or Vulkan, developers can achieve visually stunning and immersive experiences in games and applications. Each technique offers unique capabilities for enhancing realism, optimizing performance, and pushing the boundaries of graphics rendering.

Integrating Third-Party Libraries and SDKs

Integrating third-party libraries and SDKs into your C++ game development workflow can greatly enhance your project's capabilities and productivity. Below, let's discuss some popular third-party libraries and SDKs commonly used in game development, along with practical examples of how to integrate them into your C++ game project.

OpenGL / Vulkan / DirectX:

- **Description**: Graphics APIs like OpenGL, Vulkan, and DirectX provide low-level access to the GPU, enabling developers to render graphics efficiently.
- **Integration**: Include the necessary headers in your C++ files, link against the corresponding libraries, and write code to initialize the graphics context, create shaders, buffers, and textures, and issue rendering commands.

SFML (Simple and Fast Multimedia Library):

- **Description**: SFML is a multimedia library that provides simple interfaces for window creation, input handling, audio, and graphics rendering.
- **Integration**: Download the SFML library, link against it in your project, include the necessary headers, and write code to create a window, handle

input events, load and display textures, and play audio.

SDL (Simple DirectMedia Layer):

- **Description**: SDL is a cross-platform development library designed to provide low-level access to audio, keyboard, mouse, joystick, and graphics hardware.
- **Integration**: Download and install SDL, link against the SDL library in your project, include the necessary headers, and write code to initialize SDL, create a window, handle events, and render graphics.

ImGui (Dear ImGui):

- **Description**: ImGui is a bloat-free graphical user interface library for C++.
- **Integration**: Download the ImGui library, include the necessary headers in your project, and write code to create ImGui windows, draw widgets, and handle user input. ImGui is typically integrated into an existing rendering framework like OpenGL or DirectX.

Integration Example (SFML):

Below is a simple example of integrating SFML into a C++ game project:

- **Download and Install SFML**: Download the SFML library from the official website and follow the installation instructions for your development environment.
- **Link Against SFML**: In your project settings or build system configuration, link against the SFML libraries (e.g., sfml-graphics, sfml-window, sfml-system).
- **Include SFML Headers**: In your C++ source files, include the necessary SFML headers:

```cpp
#include <SFML/Graphics.hpp>
```

- **Write Code**: Write code to create a window, handle events, and render graphics using SFML:

```cpp
int main() {
    sf::RenderWindow window(sf::VideoMode(800, 600), "SFML
    Window");

    while (window.isOpen()) {
        sf::Event event;
        while (window.pollEvent(event)) {
            if (event.type == sf::Event::Closed)
                window.close();
        }

        window.clear();
        // Render graphics here
        window.display();
    }

    return 0;
}
```

- **Build and Run**: Build your project, ensuring that the SFML libraries are linked correctly, and run the executable to see the SFML window in action.

By following these steps, you can integrate SFML into your C++ game project and leverage its features for window management, input handling, and graphics rendering. Similar steps can be followed for integrating other third-party libraries and SDKs into your game development workflow.

Case Studies and Game Development Projects

Building a Simple 2D Platformer Game

Let's break down the process of building a simple 2D platformer game step by step, including the code explanations at each stage. We'll start from setting up the window and rendering a basic player character to implementing movement controls and collision detection. Let's go through each step:

Step 1: Setting up the Window

First, let's set up the window using SFML.

```cpp
#include <SFML/Graphics.hpp>

int main() {
    // Create the window
    sf::RenderWindow window(sf::VideoMode(800, 600), "Simple
    Platformer");

    // Game loop
    while (window.isOpen()) {
        // Handle events
        sf::Event event;
```

```cpp
        while (window.pollEvent(event)) {
            if (event.type == sf::Event::Closed)
                window.close();
        }


        // Clear the window
        window.clear(sf::Color::White);


        // Draw game objects


        // Display the window
        window.display();
    }

    return 0;
}
```

Explanation:

- We include the SFML/Graphics.hpp header file to use SFML graphics functionality.
- We create a window of size 800x600 pixels with the title "Simple Platformer".
- In the game loop, we handle events such as closing the window.
- We clear the window with a white color, draw game objects (which we'll add later), and display the window.

Step 2: Rendering the Player Character

Next, let's render a basic player character on the screen.

```cpp
// Inside the game loop
sf::RectangleShape player(sf::Vector2f(50.0f, 50.0f));
player.setFillColor(sf::Color::Green);
player.setPosition(100.0f, 400.0f); // Initial position
```

```
// Draw the player
window.draw(player);
```

Explanation:

- We create a sf::RectangleShape representing the player character with dimensions 50x50 pixels and color green.
- We set the initial position of the player character to (100, 400) pixels.
- Inside the game loop, we draw the player character on the window.

Step 3: Implementing Player Movement Controls

Now, let's implement basic player movement controls using the arrow keys.

```
// Inside the game loop
float playerSpeed = 5.0f;

if (sf::Keyboard::isKeyPressed(sf::Keyboard::Left)) {
    player.move(-playerSpeed, 0.0f);
} else if (sf::Keyboard::isKeyPressed(sf::Keyboard::Right)) {
    player.move(playerSpeed, 0.0f);
}

// Draw the player
window.draw(player);
```

Explanation:

- We define a playerSpeed variable to control the player's movement speed.
- Inside the game loop, we check if the left or right arrow keys are pressed.
- If the left arrow key is pressed, we move the player character left by subtracting from its x-coordinate.
- If the right arrow key is pressed, we move the player character right by adding to its x-coordinate.

Step 4: Implementing Basic Gravity and Jumping

Let's add basic gravity and jumping mechanics to the player character.

```cpp
// Inside the game loop
float gravity = 0.2f;
float jumpVelocity = -7.0f;
bool isJumping = false;

if (sf::Keyboard::isKeyPressed(sf::Keyboard::Space) &&
!isJumping) {
    playerVelocity.y = jumpVelocity;
    isJumping = true;
}

playerVelocity.y += gravity;
player.move(0.0f, playerVelocity.y);

// Check for collision with the ground (window bottom)
if (player.getPosition().y + player.getSize().y >=
window.getSize().y) {
    player.setPosition(player.getPosition().x, window.getSize().y
    - player.getSize().y);
    isJumping = false;
}

// Draw the player
window.draw(player);
```

Explanation:

- We define gravity and jumpVelocity variables to control gravity and jump strength, respectively.
- We introduce a playerVelocity.y variable to control the vertical velocity of the player character.
- When the Space key is pressed and the player is not currently jumping, we set the player's vertical velocity to jumpVelocity to make it jump.
- We simulate gravity by adding the gravity value to the player's vertical

velocity each frame.

- We move the player character vertically based on its vertical velocity.
- We check for collision with the ground (window bottom) and reset the player's position to the ground level if it reaches or goes below the ground. We also set isJumping to false to allow the player to jump again.

Step 5: Adding Platforms and Collision Detection

Finally, let's add platforms to the game and implement collision detection with the player character.

```cpp
// Define platform properties
sf::RectangleShape platform(sf::Vector2f(200.0f, 20.0f));
platform.setFillColor(sf::Color::Blue);
platform.setPosition(100.0f, 500.0f); // Example platform position

// Inside the game loop
// Check for collision with platforms
if
(player.getGlobalBounds().intersects(platform.getGlobalBounds()))
{
    player.setPosition(player.getPosition().x,
    platform.getPosition().y - player.getSize().y);
    isJumping = false;
}

// Draw platforms
window.draw(platform);
```

Explanation:

- We define a platform object with a sf::RectangleShape representing a platform with dimensions 200x20 pixels and color blue.
- Inside the game loop, we check for collision between the player character and the platform using the intersects() function.
- If a collision is detected, we reposition the player character on top of the

platform and reset the isJumping flag to allow the player to jump again.
· We draw the platforms on the window.

With these steps, we'll built a simple 2D platformer game in C++ using SFML, including setting up the window, rendering the player character, implementing movement controls, adding basic gravity and jumping mechanics, and implementing collision detection with platforms. You can further expand this game by adding more features like multiple levels, enemies, collectibles, and scoring mechanisms.

Creating the code for an entire game would be extensive, but I can provide a simplified example of a basic 2D platformer game in C++ using SFML. This example will include setting up a window, rendering a player character, implementing basic movement controls, and handling collisions with platforms.

```cpp
#include <SFML/Graphics.hpp>

int main() {
    // Create the window
    sf::RenderWindow window(sf::VideoMode(800, 600), "Simple
    Platformer");

    // Player properties
    sf::RectangleShape player(sf::Vector2f(50.0f, 50.0f));
    player.setFillColor(sf::Color::Green);
    sf::Vector2f playerVelocity(0.0f, 0.0f);
    float gravity = 0.5f;

    // Game loop
    while (window.isOpen()) {
        // Handle events
        sf::Event event;
        while (window.pollEvent(event)) {
            if (event.type == sf::Event::Closed)
                window.close();
        }
```

```cpp
// Handle player movement
if (sf::Keyboard::isKeyPressed(sf::Keyboard::Left)) {
    playerVelocity.x = -5.0f;
} else if
(sf::Keyboard::isKeyPressed(sf::Keyboard::Right)) {
    playerVelocity.x = 5.0f;
} else {
    playerVelocity.x = 0.0f;
}

// Apply gravity
playerVelocity.y += gravity;

// Update player position
player.move(playerVelocity);

// Check for collisions with window boundaries
if (player.getPosition().x < 0) {
    player.setPosition(0, player.getPosition().y);
} else if (player.getPosition().x + player.getSize().x >
window.getSize().x) {
    player.setPosition(window.getSize().x -
    player.getSize().x, player.getPosition().y);
}

if (player.getPosition().y + player.getSize().y >
window.getSize().y) {
    player.setPosition(player.getPosition().x,
    window.getSize().y - player.getSize().y);
    playerVelocity.y = 0.0f;
}

// Clear the window
window.clear();

// Draw the player
window.draw(player);

// Display the window
```

```
        window.display();
    }

    return 0;
}
```

This example sets up a simple window with a green rectangle representing the player character. The player can move left and right using the arrow keys, and gravity is applied to simulate jumping and falling. Collision detection with the window boundaries is also implemented to prevent the player from moving outside the window.

To expand the provided example into a full game, we'll add features such as level design, platforms, and collision detection with the platforms. Let's break down the steps:

Step 1: Define Platform Class

First, let's define a Platform class to represent the platforms in the game.

```
class Platform {
private:
    sf::RectangleShape shape;

public:
    Platform(float x, float y, float width, float height) {
        shape.setPosition(x, y);
        shape.setSize(sf::Vector2f(width, height));
        shape.setFillColor(sf::Color::Blue);
    }

    void draw(sf::RenderWindow& window) {
        window.draw(shape);
    }
```

```
    sf::FloatRect getGlobalBounds() const {
        return shape.getGlobalBounds();
    }
};
```

Step 2: Create Platforms

Next, let's create some platforms and store them in a vector.

```
std::vector<Platform> platforms;
platforms.push_back(Platform(0, 500, 800, 100)); // Example
platform
```

Step 3: Handle Player-Platform Collisions

Now, let's handle collisions between the player character and the platforms.

```
// Inside the game loop
for (Platform& platform : platforms) {
    if
    (player.getGlobalBounds().intersects(platform.getGlobalBounds()))
    {
        // Collision detected, move player above platform
        playerVelocity.y = 0;
        player.setPosition(player.getPosition().x,
        platform.getGlobalBounds().top - player.getSize().y);
    }
}
```

Step 4: Add Gravity and Jumping

We'll modify the gravity and jumping mechanics to only apply gravity when
the player is not on the ground and allow jumping when the player is on the
ground.

```cpp
// Inside the game loop
bool isOnGround = false;

for (Platform& platform : platforms) {
    if
    (player.getGlobalBounds().intersects(platform.getGlobalBounds()))
    {
        // Collision detected, move player above platform
        playerVelocity.y = 0;
        player.setPosition(player.getPosition().x,
        platform.getGlobalBounds().top - player.getSize().y);
        isOnGround = true;
    }
}


// Apply gravity only when not on ground
if (!isOnGround) {
    playerVelocity.y += gravity;
}


// Handle jumping
if (isOnGround &&
sf::Keyboard::isKeyPressed(sf::Keyboard::Space)) {
    playerVelocity.y = -10.0f; // Example jump velocity
}
```

Final Step: Draw Platforms and Update Player Movement

Finally, we'll draw the platforms and update the player's movement with collision detection.

```cpp
// Inside the game loop
window.clear();

// Draw platforms
for (Platform& platform : platforms) {
    platform.draw(window);
}
```

```cpp
// Update player position
player.move(playerVelocity.x, playerVelocity.y);

// Draw the player
window.draw(player);

// Display the window
window.display();
```

With these steps, we've expanded the simple platformer game example into a more complete game with platforms, collision detection, gravity, and jumping mechanics. You can further enhance the game by adding more features such as multiple levels, enemies, collectibles, and scoring.

Developing a 3D First-Person Shooter

Let's outline the steps to develop a 3D First-Person Shooter (FPS) game in C++ and include code snippets where necessary.

Step 1: Set Up the Development Environment

First, set up your development environment by installing the necessary tools and libraries. Here's a basic example using OpenGL for graphics rendering:

```cpp
#include <GL/glut.h> // Include OpenGL utility toolkit

int main(int argc, char** argv) {
    // Initialize GLUT
    glutInit(&argc, argv);
    glutInitDisplayMode(GLUT_DOUBLE | GLUT_RGB | GLUT_DEPTH);
    glutCreateWindow("3D FPS Game");

    // Set up OpenGL settings
    glEnable(GL_DEPTH_TEST);
```

```
    glEnable(GL_LIGHTING);
    glEnable(GL_LIGHT0);

    // Main game loop
    glutMainLoop();

    return 0;
}
```

Step 2: Implement Basic Game Structure

Set up the main game loop and initialize the graphics context:

```
void display() {
    // Clear color and depth buffers
    glClear(GL_COLOR_BUFFER_BIT | GL_DEPTH_BUFFER_BIT);

    // Set up camera/viewpoint
    glMatrixMode(GL_MODELVIEW);
    glLoadIdentity();
    gluLookAt(0.0, 0.0, 5.0, 0.0, 0.0, 0.0, 0.0, 1.0, 0.0);

    // Render game objects
    // Add code to render 3D models, environments, etc.

    // Swap buffers
    glutSwapBuffers();
}

int main(int argc, char** argv) {
    // Initialize GLUT
    glutInit(&argc, argv);
    glutInitDisplayMode(GLUT_DOUBLE | GLUT_RGB | GLUT_DEPTH);
    glutCreateWindow("3D FPS Game");

    // Set up OpenGL settings
    glEnable(GL_DEPTH_TEST);
    glEnable(GL_LIGHTING);
```

```cpp
    glEnable(GL_LIGHT0);

    // Register display callback function
    glutDisplayFunc(display);

    // Main game loop
    glutMainLoop();

    return 0;
}
```

Step 3: Implement Player Controls

Implement player movement and controls using keyboard and mouse input:

```cpp
// Global variables for player position
float playerX = 0.0f;
float playerY = 0.0f;
float playerZ = 0.0f;

void keyboard(unsigned char key, int x, int y) {
    switch (key) {
        case 'w':
            playerZ -= 0.1f; // Move player forward
            break;
        case 's':
            playerZ += 0.1f; // Move player backward
            break;
        // Add more controls for movement, shooting, etc.
    }
    glutPostRedisplay(); // Trigger display update
}

int main(int argc, char** argv) {
    // Initialize GLUT
    glutInit(&argc, argv);
    glutInitDisplayMode(GLUT_DOUBLE | GLUT_RGB | GLUT_DEPTH);
    glutCreateWindow("3D FPS Game");
```

```
    // Set up OpenGL settings
    glEnable(GL_DEPTH_TEST);
    glEnable(GL_LIGHTING);
    glEnable(GL_LIGHT0);

    // Register display callback function
    glutDisplayFunc(display);

    // Register keyboard callback function
    glutKeyboardFunc(keyboard);

    // Main game loop
    glutMainLoop();

    return 0;
}
```

Step 4: Implement Enemy AI

Add enemy AI behavior, such as patrolling, detecting the player, and attacking:

```
// Define Enemy class with AI behavior
class Enemy {
public:
    void patrol() {
        // Implement patrol behavior
    }

    void detectPlayer() {
        // Implement player detection logic
    }

    void attackPlayer() {
        // Implement attack behavior
    }
};
```

```cpp
// Main game loop
void update() {
    // Update enemy AI behavior
    enemy.patrol();
    enemy.detectPlayer();
    enemy.attackPlayer();
}
```

Step 5: Add Weapons and Combat Mechanics

Implement weapon systems, shooting mechanics, and damage calculation:

```cpp
class Weapon {
public:
    void shoot() {
        // Implement shooting behavior
    }
};

// Main game loop
void update() {
    // Update player and enemy actions
    player.update();
    enemy.update();

    // Handle shooting
    if (isShooting) {
        weapon.shoot();
    }
}
```

Step 6: Implement Game HUD and UI

Design and implement the HUD elements, such as health bars and ammo counters:

```cpp
void drawHUD() {
    // Draw HUD elements using OpenGL
}

void display() {
    // Clear color and depth buffers
    glClear(GL_COLOR_BUFFER_BIT | GL_DEPTH_BUFFER_BIT);

    // Set up camera/viewpoint
    glMatrixMode(GL_MODELVIEW);
    glLoadIdentity();
    gluLookAt(0.0, 0.0, 5.0, 0.0, 0.0, 0.0, 0.0, 1.0, 0.0);

    // Render game objects
    // ...

    // Draw HUD
    drawHUD();

    // Swap buffers
    glutSwapBuffers();
}
```

Step 7: Test, Optimize, and Polish

Test the game thoroughly, optimize performance, and polish the graphics, controls, and gameplay mechanics for a better player experience.

By following these steps and integrating the provided code snippets, you can start developing a basic 3D FPS game in C++. Remember to continuously iterate on your design, gather feedback, and refine your implementation to create an engaging and enjoyable gaming experience.

Below is a simplified example of a basic 3D FPS game using OpenGL for rendering and GLUT for window management. This example includes player movement, basic shooting mechanics, and rendering a simple environment with walls and obstacles.

```cpp
#include <GL/glut.h> // Include OpenGL utility toolkit
#include <iostream>

// Define constants
const int WINDOW_WIDTH = 800;
const int WINDOW_HEIGHT = 600;
const float PLAYER_SPEED = 0.1f;
const float BULLET_SPEED = 0.5f;

// Player variables
float playerX = 0.0f;
float playerY = 0.0f;
float playerZ = 0.0f;
float playerAngle = 0.0f;

// Bullet variables
bool isShooting = false;
float bulletX = 0.0f;
float bulletY = 0.0f;
float bulletZ = 0.0f;

void drawPlayer() {
    glPushMatrix();
    glTranslatef(playerX, playerY, playerZ);
    glRotatef(playerAngle, 0.0f, 1.0f, 0.0f);
    glColor3f(1.0f, 0.0f, 0.0f); // Red color for player
    glutSolidCube(1.0f); // Player model (cube)
    glPopMatrix();
}

void drawBullet() {
    if (isShooting) {
        glPushMatrix();
        glColor3f(0.0f, 1.0f, 0.0f); // Green color for bullets
        glTranslatef(bulletX, bulletY, bulletZ);
        glutSolidSphere(0.05f, 10, 10); // Bullet model (sphere)
        glPopMatrix();
    }
```

```c
}

void display() {
    glClear(GL_COLOR_BUFFER_BIT | GL_DEPTH_BUFFER_BIT);
    glLoadIdentity();

    // Set up camera/viewpoint
    gluLookAt(playerX, playerY + 0.5f, playerZ - 1.0f,
              playerX, playerY, playerZ,
              0.0f, 1.0f, 0.0f);

    drawPlayer();
    drawBullet();

    glutSwapBuffers();
}

void keyboard(unsigned char key, int x, int y) {
    switch (key) {
        case 'w':
            playerZ -= PLAYER_SPEED;
            break;
        case 's':
            playerZ += PLAYER_SPEED;
            break;
        case 'a':
            playerAngle += 2.0f;
            break;
        case 'd':
            playerAngle -= 2.0f;
            break;
        case ' ':
            isShooting = true;
            bulletX = playerX;
            bulletY = playerY;
            bulletZ = playerZ;
            break;
        case 27: // ESC key
            exit(0);
            break;
```

```cpp
    }
    glutPostRedisplay();
}


void update(int value) {
    if (isShooting) {
        bulletZ += BULLET_SPEED;
        if (bulletZ > 50.0f) {
            isShooting = false;
        }
    }
    glutTimerFunc(10, update, 0);
}


int main(int argc, char** argv) {
    glutInit(&argc, argv);
    glutInitDisplayMode(GLUT_DOUBLE | GLUT_RGB | GLUT_DEPTH);
    glutInitWindowSize(WINDOW_WIDTH, WINDOW_HEIGHT);
    glutCreateWindow("3D FPS Game");

    glEnable(GL_DEPTH_TEST);

    glutDisplayFunc(display);
    glutKeyboardFunc(keyboard);

    glutTimerFunc(10, update, 0);

    glutMainLoop();
    return 0;
}
```

This code creates a basic 3D FPS game window using OpenGL and GLUT. The player can move forward and backward (w, s keys) and rotate left and right (a, d keys). Pressing the spacebar shoots a bullet from the player's current position.

To expand this example into a full-fledged game, you'll need to add features such as enemy AI, level design, weapon mechanics, sound effects, and more sophisticated graphics. Additionally, you may consider using a game engine like Unity or Unreal Engine for more advanced game development.

Creating a Multiplayer Online Battle Arena (MOBA) Game

Creating a Multiplayer Online Battle Arena (MOBA) game involves developing a complex system that includes player-controlled characters, AI-controlled minions, a map with obstacles and objectives, networking for multiplayer functionality, and game mechanics such as abilities, items, and victory conditions. Let's break down the key components and considerations for developing a MOBA game, along with relevant code snippets.

Game Structure and Mechanics

A MOBA game typically consists of two teams of players competing against each other to destroy the opposing team's base while defending their own. Players control unique characters with different abilities and roles, such as tanks, damage dealers, and support characters. The game map is divided into lanes, and each team spawns minions that automatically advance along the lanes to attack enemy structures and players.

Networking for Multiplayer

Networking is crucial for implementing multiplayer functionality in a MOBA game. You'll need to set up a client-server architecture to handle communication between players and synchronize game state across all clients. Use a reliable networking library such as RakNet or ENet to manage network connections, message serialization, and data transfer between clients and the server.

Player and Character Control

Implement player input handling to control character movement, abilities, and interactions. Use a finite state machine (FSM) to manage character states such as idle, moving, attacking, and using abilities. Ensure smooth and responsive controls by implementing client-side prediction and server reconciliation to compensate for network latency and ensure consistent gameplay experience across all clients.

AI for Minions and NPCs

Develop AI routines to control minions and neutral monsters on the map. Minions should follow predefined paths along the lanes, prioritize targets based on proximity and threat level, and engage in combat with enemy minions and players. Neutral monsters can provide additional objectives and rewards for players who defeat them, encouraging strategic map control and teamwork.

Game Map and Objectives

Design and implement the game map with lanes, jungle areas, and strategic objectives such as towers, inhibitors, and the central base. Use data structures like graphs or tilemaps to represent the map layout and navigation paths. Define victory conditions and game progression mechanics, such as destroying enemy structures to advance toward the enemy base and ultimately win the game.

Abilities, Items, and Progression

Create a variety of unique abilities and items for player characters to customize their playstyle and adapt to different situations. Abilities can include offensive skills, defensive abilities, crowd control effects, and utility spells. Implement a progression system to allow players to level up their characters, unlock new abilities, and purchase items to enhance their stats and abilities during the game.

Code Example: Player Movement

```
void handlePlayerMovement(Player player, Vector2D direction) {
    // Update player position based on input direction
    player.move(direction * player.getSpeed());

    // Send player movement data to server for synchronization
    NetworkManager.sendPlayerMovementData(player.getID(),
    player.getPosition());
}
```

Code Example: Minion AI

```
void updateMinionAI(Minion minion) {
    if (minion.getState() == State::Idle) {
        // Find nearest enemy target
        GameObject target =
        findNearestEnemy(minion.getPosition());

        // If target found, switch to attack state
        if (target != nullptr) {
            minion.setState(State::Attack);
            minion.setTarget(target);
        }
    }
    else if (minion.getState() == State::Attack) {
        // Move towards target and attack
        minion.moveTowards(minion.getTarget().getPosition());
        minion.attack(minion.getTarget());
    }
}
```

Code Example: Networking

```
void handleNetworkMessages() {
    while (NetworkManager.hasPendingMessages()) {
        Message msg = NetworkManager.getNextMessage();

        switch (msg.getType()) {
```

```cpp
        case MessageType::PlayerMovement:
            // Update player position based on received data
            updatePlayerPosition(msg.getPlayerID(),
            msg.getPosition());
            break;
        // Handle other message types (e.g., ability usage,
        game events)
    }
  }
}
```

Developing a MOBA game is a complex and challenging endeavor that requires careful planning, iterative development, and attention to detail. By focusing on the key components outlined above and leveraging suitable libraries and frameworks, you can create an immersive and engaging multiplayer experience for players to enjoy.

Conclusion and Next Steps

Recap of Key Learnings

Through our exploration of C++ game development, we've delved into fundamental concepts and techniques essential for building immersive gaming experiences. We began by understanding the foundational structure of games, grasping the intricacies of the game loop, which orchestrates input handling, state updates, and graphical rendering. This understanding laid the groundwork for our subsequent endeavors.

Graphics rendering emerged as a critical aspect of game development, prompting us to harness the power of graphics libraries like SFML or OpenGL to bring our virtual worlds to life. With these tools, we learned to craft visually captivating scenes, integrating sprites, shapes, and textures to create engaging gameplay environments.

Central to player engagement is the seamless integration of player input mechanisms. We dived into the intricacies of input handling, mastering the art of translating player actions from keyboard, mouse, or gamepad into meaningful interactions within the game world. This mastery empowered us to create responsive and intuitive gameplay experiences.

Venturing into multiplayer functionality, we embarked on the journey of networking in games. We navigated the complexities of client-server communication, crafting robust systems that enable real-time interaction between players across the vast expanse of the internet. This exploration expanded our horizons, opening doors to the realm of multiplayer gaming.

As our understanding deepened, we delved into the realm of game physics, mastering the principles that govern motion, collision, and interaction within virtual environments. Armed with this knowledge, we imbued our games with realistic dynamics, enhancing immersion and believability.

At the heart of our development journey lies the principles of Object-Oriented Programming (OOP). Through the lens of OOP, we organized our code into modular, reusable components, fostering maintainability and scalability. This architectural approach empowered us to navigate the complexities of game development with confidence and clarity.

Throughout our odyssey, we honed our skills in data structures and algorithms, leveraging these foundational tools to tackle a myriad of game development challenges. From pathfinding algorithms to data storage and retrieval mechanisms, these tools served as invaluable allies in our quest for mastery.

In the pursuit of excellence, we embraced game design patterns, leveraging tried and tested solutions to common development challenges. These patterns, ranging from the observer pattern to the state pattern, endowed our code with elegance and flexibility, paving the way for sustainable development practices.

With an unwavering commitment to optimization, we fine-tuned our games for performance, meticulously optimizing rendering pipelines, memory usage, and algorithmic efficiency. Through diligent testing and debugging, we identified and rectified issues, ensuring a polished and seamless player experience.

As our journey draws to a close, we stand on the precipice of possibility, armed with the knowledge, skills, and passion to embark on new adventures in the dynamic realm of C++ game development. With each challenge overcome and lesson learned, we emerge stronger, more capable, and ready to shape the future of interactive entertainment.

Further Resources for Game Development

For aspiring game developers seeking to deepen their expertise in C++, a wealth of further resources awaits. Online communities such as forums, subreddits, and Discord servers offer invaluable opportunities to connect with fellow developers, seek advice, and share insights. Websites like Stack Overflow and GameDev.net serve as hubs for knowledge exchange, housing vast repositories of Q&A threads, tutorials, and articles on game development topics.

For those craving structured learning experiences, online platforms like Udemy, Coursera, and Udacity offer a plethora of courses tailored to various skill levels and interests. From beginner-friendly introductions to advanced topics in graphics programming, artificial intelligence, and multiplayer networking, these courses provide comprehensive guidance and hands-on practice.

The world of game development literature abounds with timeless classics and modern gems alike. Books such as "Game Programming Patterns" by Robert Nystrom, "Effective C++" by Scott Meyers, and "OpenGL Programming Guide" by Dave Shreiner offer invaluable insights into game design principles, best practices in C++ programming, and graphics programming fundamentals.

For those seeking real-world examples and practical guidance, studying open-source game projects on platforms like GitHub can prove immensely beneficial. Analyzing the source code of popular game engines like Unreal

Engine and Godot Engine, as well as community-driven projects, provides invaluable insights into industry-standard practices, architecture design, and optimization techniques.

Attending game development conferences, workshops, and hackathons offers unparalleled opportunities to network with industry professionals, collaborate on projects, and gain hands-on experience. Events like the Game Developers Conference (GDC), Global Game Jam (GGJ), and Ludum Dare provide fertile grounds for creativity, innovation, and community building.

Next Steps in Your Game Development Journey

As you venture forward in your game development journey, consider the following pathways to deepen your expertise and broaden your horizons:

Explore Specializations: Identify areas within game development that captivate your interest, whether it's graphics programming, artificial intelligence, networking, or game design. By focusing on specific domains, you can delve deeper into their intricacies and master their nuances.

Advance Your Skills: Embrace advanced topics in C++ game development, such as multithreading, advanced graphics techniques like ray tracing, sophisticated networking protocols such as UDP or WebSockets, or procedural content generation algorithms.

Experiment with Game Engines: Familiarize yourself with popular game engines like Unity or Unreal Engine. Experiment with these engines to understand their workflows, tools, and capabilities, unlocking new possibilities for creating immersive experiences.

Collaborate and Connect: Engage with game development communities, forums, and online platforms to collaborate with fellow developers, share insights, and receive feedback on your projects. Collaborative endeavors foster learning, growth, and the cultivation of a supportive network within the industry.

Craft Your Portfolio: Curate a portfolio showcasing your game projects to demonstrate your skills and accomplishments to potential employers or collaborators. Craft polished, playable demos that showcase your strengths and creativity as a game developer.

Embrace Lifelong Learning: Stay abreast of industry trends, emerging technologies, and best practices in game development through continuous learning. Stay curious, explore new ideas, and remain adaptable in an ever-evolving landscape.

Define Your Career Path: Reflect on your aspirations within the game development field, whether it's pursuing a career at a game studio, becoming an independent developer, or exploring opportunities in academia. Define your goals and take deliberate steps towards realizing them.

Cultivate Passion Projects: Dedicate time to work on passion projects that ignite your creativity and fuel your enthusiasm for game development. Whether it's a small indie game, a game jam entry, or an experimental project, these endeavors offer opportunities for growth and self-expression.

Forge Ahead: Embrace challenges, celebrate achievements, and remain resilient in the face of obstacles. Game development is a journey of continual growth and discovery, and each step forward brings new opportunities for innovation and fulfillment.

III

Core Game Development Techniques

Graphics Rendering with OpenGL

Graphics rendering with OpenGL provides a powerful framework for creating visually stunning and interactive 2D and 3D graphics in real-time applications. OpenGL, or Open Graphics Library, is a cross-platform API that enables developers to harness the full potential of modern graphics hardware to render scenes with high fidelity and performance. At its core, OpenGL operates by defining a series of rendering commands and passing them to the GPU for execution, allowing for efficient parallel processing and rendering of complex scenes.

One of the key strengths of OpenGL lies in its support for hardware acceleration, leveraging the capabilities of dedicated graphics processing units (GPUs) to perform computationally intensive tasks such as vertex transformations, rasterization, and fragment shading. By offloading these tasks to the GPU, OpenGL enables developers to achieve smooth, high-speed rendering of dynamic scenes with realistic lighting, shadows, and textures, enhancing the immersive quality of interactive applications.

OpenGL's flexible architecture and extensive feature set make it well-suited for a wide range of graphics applications, from simple 2D games to sophisticated 3D simulations and visualizations. Developers have access to a rich set of rendering primitives, shaders, and advanced rendering techniques, empowering them to create visually compelling experiences tailored to the specific requirements of their projects. Whether building immersive virtual worlds, educational simulations, or data visualization tools, OpenGL provides the tools and capabilities needed to bring creative visions to life with unparalleled visual fidelity and performance.

Introduction to OpenGL

OpenGL, or Open Graphics Library, serves as a powerful cross-platform API for rendering 2D and 3D graphics in real-time applications. As a standard specification, it enables developers to interact with graphics hardware, accessing features and capabilities for creating immersive visual experiences. Here's a detailed overview of OpenGL:

- **Platform Independence**: OpenGL is platform-independent, meaning it can be used across various operating systems, including Windows, macOS, and Linux, providing flexibility and portability for developers.
- **Rendering Pipeline**: OpenGL follows a programmable rendering pipeline, consisting of stages such as vertex processing, primitive assembly, rasterization, and fragment processing. Developers can customize and optimize each stage to achieve desired rendering effects.
- **Graphics Primitives**: OpenGL supports rendering of various graphics primitives, including points, lines, and polygons. These primitives serve as the building blocks for creating complex 2D and 3D scenes.
- **Shader Programming**: Modern OpenGL versions utilize shader programs written in languages like GLSL (OpenGL Shading Language) to define how vertices and fragments are processed. Developers can write custom shaders to implement advanced rendering techniques such as lighting, shadows, and post-processing effects.
- **Buffer Objects**: OpenGL provides buffer objects to efficiently store and manipulate data on the GPU. Vertex Buffer Objects (VBOs) and Index Buffer Objects (IBOs) are commonly used to store vertex data and index data, respectively, for rendering geometry.
- **Texture Mapping**: Texture mapping allows developers to apply textures to surfaces in 3D scenes, enhancing realism and detail. OpenGL supports various texture types, including 1D, 2D, and 3D textures, as well as texture

mapping modes and filtering options.

Example Code: Below is a simple example of initializing an OpenGL context and rendering a colored triangle using modern OpenGL (OpenGL 3.3 and above) with GLFW and GLEW libraries in C++:

```cpp
#include <GL/glew.h>
#include <GLFW/glfw3.h>
#include <iostream>

void render() {
    glClear(GL_COLOR_BUFFER_BIT);

    glBegin(GL_TRIANGLES);
    glColor3f(1.0f, 0.0f, 0.0f);
    glVertex2f(-0.5f, -0.5f);
    glColor3f(0.0f, 1.0f, 0.0f);
    glVertex2f(0.5f, -0.5f);
    glColor3f(0.0f, 0.0f, 1.0f);
    glVertex2f(0.0f, 0.5f);
    glEnd();
}

int main() {
    // Initialize GLFW
    if (!glfwInit()) {
        std::cerr << "Failed to initialize GLFW" << std::endl;
        return -1;
    }

    // Create a GLFW window
    GLFWwindow* window = glfwCreateWindow(800, 600, "OpenGL
Window", nullptr, nullptr);
    if (!window) {
        std::cerr << "Failed to create GLFW window" << std::endl;
        glfwTerminate();
        return -1;
    }
```

```cpp
    // Make the window's context current
    glfwMakeContextCurrent(window);

    // Initialize GLEW
    if (glewInit() != GLEW_OK) {
        std::cerr << "Failed to initialize GLEW" << std::endl;
        return -1;
    }

    // Loop until the user closes the window
    while (!glfwWindowShouldClose(window)) {
        // Render
        render();

        // Swap front and back buffers
        glfwSwapBuffers(window);

        // Poll for and process events
        glfwPollEvents();
    }

    // Terminate GLFW
    glfwTerminate();

    return 0;
}
```

This code initializes an OpenGL context using GLFW, creates a window, and renders a colored triangle using immediate mode rendering. However, immediate mode rendering is deprecated in modern OpenGL in favor of using vertex buffer objects and shader programs for improved performance and flexibility.

Setting Up OpenGL Environment

Setting up an OpenGL environment involves configuring the necessary libraries and tools to begin developing OpenGL applications. Below is a step-by-step guide, including C++ code where applicable:

Install Necessary Libraries:

- Download and install OpenGL libraries such as GLFW (OpenGL Framework), GLEW (OpenGL Extension Wrangler Library), and GLM (OpenGL Mathematics).
- Use a package manager like **apt**, **brew**, or download from official websites.

Set Up Development Environment:

- Create a new C++ project in your preferred IDE (Integrated Development Environment) or text editor.
- Include necessary OpenGL headers and link the OpenGL libraries in your project settings.

Initialize GLFW:

- Use GLFW to create an OpenGL context and manage windows.
- Here's an example of initializing GLFW in C++:

```cpp
#include <GLFW/glfw3.h>

int main() {
    // Initialize GLFW
    if (!glfwInit()) {
        // Error handling
        return -1;
    }

    // GLFW initialization succeeded
    // Further OpenGL setup can be done here

    return 0;
}
```

Create a Window:

- Use GLFW to create a window for OpenGL rendering.
- Set the window size, title, and other properties.
- Here's an example of creating a window with GLFW:

```cpp
#include <GLFW/glfw3.h>

int main() {
    // Initialize GLFW
    if (!glfwInit()) {
        // Error handling
        return -1;
    }

    // Create a windowed mode window and its OpenGL context
    GLFWwindow* window = glfwCreateWindow(800, 600, "OpenGL
    Window", nullptr, nullptr);
    if (!window) {
        // Error handling
        glfwTerminate();
        return -1;
    }

    // Make the window's context current
    glfwMakeContextCurrent(window);

    // Loop until the user closes the window
    while (!glfwWindowShouldClose(window)) {
        // Render OpenGL scene
        // ...

        // Swap front and back buffers
        glfwSwapBuffers(window);

        // Poll for and process events
        glfwPollEvents();
    }

    // Terminate GLFW
```

```
    glfwTerminate();

    return 0;
}
```

Render OpenGL Scene:

- Implement rendering code to draw graphics using OpenGL commands.
- This typically involves clearing the screen, setting up projection and view matrices, and rendering geometry and textures.
- We can't include a full rendering example here due to space limitations, but basic rendering involves using OpenGL functions like **glClear()**, **glMatrixMode()**, **glLoadIdentity()**, **glBegin()**, **glEnd()**, etc.

Clean Up:

- Properly clean up resources and terminate GLFW after use.
- This ensures a graceful exit and prevents resource leaks.

Compile and Run:

- Compile your C++ code with appropriate compiler flags to link OpenGL libraries.
- Run the executable to see the OpenGL window and rendering in action.

Setting up an OpenGL environment in C++ is the first step towards creating interactive graphics applications. With the environment configured, you can begin exploring OpenGL's vast capabilities and unleash your creativity in graphics programming.

Rendering 2D and 3D Graphics

To render 2D and 3D graphics using OpenGL in C++, we'll first set up a basic OpenGL environment and then create examples for rendering both 2D and 3D graphics.

Setting Up OpenGL Environment:

```cpp
#include <GL/glew.h>
#include <GLFW/glfw3.h>
#include <iostream>

int main() {
    // Initialize GLFW
    if (!glfwInit()) {
        std::cerr << "Failed to initialize GLFW" << std::endl;
        return -1;
    }

    // Create a GLFW window
    GLFWwindow* window = glfwCreateWindow(800, 600, "OpenGL
    Window", nullptr, nullptr);
    if (!window) {
        std::cerr << "Failed to create GLFW window" << std::endl;
        glfwTerminate();
        return -1;
    }

    // Make the window's context current
    glfwMakeContextCurrent(window);

    // Initialize GLEW
    if (glewInit() != GLEW_OK) {
        std::cerr << "Failed to initialize GLEW" << std::endl;
        return -1;
    }

    // Loop until the user closes the window
```

```cpp
    while (!glfwWindowShouldClose(window)) {
        // Render OpenGL scene
        // ...

        // Swap front and back buffers
        glfwSwapBuffers(window);

        // Poll for and process events
        glfwPollEvents();
    }

    // Terminate GLFW
    glfwTerminate();

    return 0;
}
```

Rendering 2D Graphics (Drawing a Rectangle):

```cpp
#include <GL/glew.h>
#include <GLFW/glfw3.h>
#include <iostream>

void render() {
    glClear(GL_COLOR_BUFFER_BIT);

    glBegin(GL_QUADS);
    glColor3f(1.0f, 0.0f, 0.0f); // Red color
    glVertex2f(-0.5f, -0.5f);    // Bottom-left corner
    glVertex2f(0.5f, -0.5f);     // Bottom-right corner
    glVertex2f(0.5f, 0.5f);      // Top-right corner
    glVertex2f(-0.5f, 0.5f);     // Top-left corner
    glEnd();
}

int main() {
    // Initialize GLFW and GLEW (same as before)

    while (!glfwWindowShouldClose(window)) {
```

```cpp
        // Render 2D graphics
        render();

        // Swap front and back buffers, poll for events (same as
        before)
    }

    // Terminate GLFW (same as before)

    return 0;
}
```

Rendering 3D Graphics (Drawing a Cube):

```cpp
#include <GL/glew.h>
#include <GLFW/glfw3.h>
#include <iostream>

void render() {
    glClear(GL_COLOR_BUFFER_BIT | GL_DEPTH_BUFFER_BIT);

    glBegin(GL_QUADS);

    // Front face
    glColor3f(1.0f, 0.0f, 0.0f); // Red color
    glVertex3f(-0.5f, -0.5f, 0.5f); // Bottom-left corner
    glVertex3f(0.5f, -0.5f, 0.5f);  // Bottom-right corner
    glVertex3f(0.5f, 0.5f, 0.5f);   // Top-right corner
    glVertex3f(-0.5f, 0.5f, 0.5f);  // Top-left corner

    // Back face
    // (Similar vertices with different z-coordinates)

    glEnd();
}

int main() {
    // Initialize GLFW and GLEW (same as before)
```

```
glEnable(GL_DEPTH_TEST); // Enable depth testing for 3D
rendering

while (!glfwWindowShouldClose(window)) {
    // Render 3D graphics
    render();

    // Swap front and back buffers, poll for events (same as
    before)
}

// Terminate GLFW (same as before)

return 0;
}
```

In the 2D graphics example, we draw a simple red rectangle using **GL_QUADS**. Each **glVertex2f** call specifies a vertex with x and y coordinates, forming the corners of the rectangle.

In the 3D graphics example, we draw a cube by specifying vertices for each face using **glVertex3f**, which includes x, y, and z coordinates. We enable depth testing (**GL_DEPTH_TEST**) to ensure proper rendering of 3D objects based on their distance from the camera.

Game Physics and Collision Detection

Game physics and collision detection are essential components of interactive game worlds, responsible for simulating realistic interactions between objects and environments. At the core of game physics lies the simulation of physical laws and principles, such as gravity, friction, and inertia, to create believable movement and dynamics. By accurately modeling these phenomena, game developers can imbue virtual worlds with a sense of realism and immersion, enhancing the player experience.

Collision detection is a fundamental aspect of game physics, enabling games to determine when objects intersect or come into contact with each other. Whether it's a player character colliding with obstacles, projectiles hitting targets, or vehicles crashing into obstacles, collision detection algorithms play a crucial role in enforcing game rules and mechanics. These algorithms range from simple bounding box checks to more complex geometric calculations, depending on the level of precision required and the complexity of the game environment.

Incorporating robust collision detection and physics simulation into game development requires careful consideration of performance, accuracy, and scalability. Game developers must strike a balance between computational efficiency and accuracy, optimizing collision detection algorithms to handle large numbers of objects in real-time. Additionally, developers may leverage physics engines and libraries, such as Box2D or Bullet, to streamline the implementation of physics simulations and collision detection, allowing them to focus on game design and content creation.

Implementing Physics in Games

Implementing physics in games using C++ involves simulating the behavior of objects based on real-world physical principles such as gravity, friction, and collisions. Below, I'll outline the basic steps involved in implementing physics in a game, along with code examples and explanations where applicable:

Define Physics Properties:

- Define properties such as mass, velocity, acceleration, and forces for game objects.
- These properties will govern the movement and behavior of objects in the game world.

Update Object Positions:

- Implement a function to update the positions of game objects based on their velocities and accelerations.
- This function should be called each frame to simulate continuous movement.

Example Code for Updating Object Positions:

```
void updatePosition(GameObject& obj, float deltaTime) {
    // Update velocity based on acceleration
    obj.velocity += obj.acceleration * deltaTime;

    // Update position based on velocity
    obj.position += obj.velocity * deltaTime;
}
```

Apply Forces:

- Apply forces such as gravity, friction, and user input to game objects.
- Forces can be accumulated and applied to objects during the position update step.

Example Code for Applying Gravity:

```cpp
const float GRAVITY = 9.81f;

void applyGravity(GameObject& obj) {
    obj.acceleration.y -= GRAVITY;
}
```

Detect Collisions:

- Implement collision detection algorithms to detect when objects intersect or come into contact with each other.
- Depending on the type of game and objects involved, use appropriate collision detection techniques such as bounding boxes, bounding spheres, or more complex geometric algorithms.

Example Code for Simple Bounding Box Collision Detection:

```cpp
bool checkCollision(const GameObject& obj1, const GameObject&
obj2) {
    // Check if bounding boxes of obj1 and obj2 overlap
    return (obj1.position.x < obj2.position.x + obj2.size.x &&
            obj1.position.x + obj1.size.x > obj2.position.x &&
            obj1.position.y < obj2.position.y + obj2.size.y &&
            obj1.position.y + obj1.size.y > obj2.position.y);
}
```

Resolve Collisions:

- If a collision is detected, implement collision resolution techniques to handle the interaction between objects.

- Depending on the game mechanics, this may involve bouncing off objects, applying forces, or triggering game events.

Example Code for Bouncing Off Objects:

```cpp
void resolveCollision(GameObject& obj1, GameObject& obj2) {
    // Reverse velocities of obj1 and obj2 to simulate bouncing
    off
    obj1.velocity *= -1.0f;
    obj2.velocity *= -1.0f;
}
```

By following these steps and incorporating appropriate code examples, developers can effectively implement physics in games using C++, creating dynamic and engaging gameplay experiences.

Understanding Collision Detection Algorithms

Collision detection algorithms are fundamental in game development, enabling games to detect when objects intersect or come into contact with each other. Below, I'll discuss common collision detection algorithms and provide code examples to illustrate their implementation:

Bounding Box Collision Detection:

- Bounding box collision detection involves representing objects as axis-aligned bounding boxes (AABBs) and checking if these boxes intersect.

Example Code for Bounding Box Collision Detection:

```cpp
bool checkBoundingBoxCollision(const AABB& box1, const AABB&
box2) {
    // Check if bounding boxes of box1 and box2 overlap
    return (box1.minX < box2.maxX && box1.maxX > box2.minX &&
```

```
        box1.minY < box2.maxY && box1.maxY > box2.minY &&
        box1.minZ < box2.maxZ && box1.maxZ > box2.minZ);
}
```

Bounding Sphere Collision Detection:

- Bounding sphere collision detection involves representing objects as spheres and checking if the distance between their centers is less than the sum of their radii.

Example Code for Bounding Sphere Collision Detection:

```
bool checkBoundingSphereCollision(const Sphere& sphere1, const
Sphere& sphere2) {
    // Calculate distance between sphere centers
    float distance = glm::distance(sphere1.center,
    sphere2.center);

    // Check if distance is less than sum of radii
    return (distance < sphere1.radius + sphere2.radius);
}
```

Ray Casting:

- Ray casting involves casting a ray from one object to another and checking if it intersects with any obstacles along the way.

Example Code for Ray Casting:

```
bool rayIntersectsObstacle(const Ray& ray, const Obstacle&
obstacle) {
    // Calculate intersection point of ray with obstacle
    Vector3 intersectionPoint = ray.origin + ray.direction * t;

    // Check if intersection point is inside obstacle bounds
```

```
    return (intersectionPoint.x >= obstacle.minX &&
    intersectionPoint.x <= obstacle.maxX &&
         intersectionPoint.y >= obstacle.minY &&
         intersectionPoint.y <= obstacle.maxY &&
         intersectionPoint.z >= obstacle.minZ &&
         intersectionPoint.z <= obstacle.maxZ);
}
```

Separating Axis Theorem (SAT):

- SAT is used for collision detection between convex polygons or polyhedra by checking if there exists a separating axis between them.

Example Code for SAT Collision Detection:

```
bool checkSATCollision(const ConvexPolygon& poly1, const
ConvexPolygon& poly2) {
    // Project polygons onto potential separating axes
    for (const Vector2& axis : poly1.axes) {
        // Project polygons onto axis
        float min1 = poly1.getMinProjection(axis);
        float max1 = poly1.getMaxProjection(axis);
        float min2 = poly2.getMinProjection(axis);
        float max2 = poly2.getMaxProjection(axis);

        // Check for overlap
        if (max1 < min2 || max2 < min1) {
            // Separating axis found
            return false;
        }
    }
    // No separating axis found, collision detected
    return true;
}
```

Collision Detection Algorithms strengths and weaknesses

Collision detection algorithms play a crucial role in game development, but each algorithm has its own strengths and weaknesses, which determine its suitability for different scenarios. Here's an overview of the strengths and weaknesses of common collision detection algorithms:

Bounding Box Collision Detection:
  Strengths:

- Simple and efficient to implement.
- Provides a quick first-pass check for potential collisions.
- Works well for objects with regular shapes or uniform dimensions.

Weaknesses:

- May produce false positives or false negatives for objects with irregular shapes.
- Inaccurate for objects with significant empty space within their bounding boxes.
- Requires additional checks for precise collision detection.

Bounding Sphere Collision Detection:
  Strengths:

- More accurate than bounding boxes for objects with irregular shapes.
- Provides a quick approximation of collision detection.
- Works well for objects with varying sizes and shapes.

Weaknesses:

- Less accurate than other algorithms for objects with complex geometry.
- May not detect collisions accurately for objects with elongated or asymmetric shapes.
- Requires more computational resources for objects with many overlapping spheres.

Ray Casting:

Strengths:

- Provides precise collision detection along a specified direction or path.
- Suitable for detecting collisions with thin or irregularly shaped objects.
- Allows for dynamic detection of obstacles or targets in the game environment.

Weaknesses:

- Can be computationally expensive, especially for complex scenes with many obstacles.
- Requires careful handling of intersections and edge cases.
- Limited to detecting collisions along the path of the ray, may miss collisions outside its trajectory.

Separating Axis Theorem (SAT):

Strengths:

- Provides precise collision detection for convex polygons or polyhedra.
- Guarantees accurate detection of collisions between objects with complex shapes.
- Works well for detecting collisions between moving objects.

Weaknesses:

- More complex to implement compared to bounding box or sphere collision detection.
- Requires additional pre-processing to compute separating axes for each object.
- Inefficient for detecting collisions between objects with many vertices or intricate geometry.

Overall, the choice of collision detection algorithm depends on factors such as the complexity of the game environment, the shapes of the objects involved, performance requirements, and the desired level of accuracy. Often, a combination of different algorithms is used to achieve efficient and accurate collision detection in games.

By understanding and implementing these algorithms, developers can create robust collision detection systems for their games, ensuring realistic interactions between objects in the game world.

Integrating Physics Engine into Your Game

Integrating a physics engine into a game involves incorporating a library or framework that provides physics simulation capabilities, such as rigid body dynamics, collision detection, and force propagation. One popular physics engine used in game development is Box2D. Below, I'll outline the steps to integrate Box2D into a game and provide code examples where necessary:

Download and Setup Box2D:

Download the Box2D library from the official repository or package manager. Include the necessary headers in your project and link against the Box2D library.

Initialize Box2D World:

Create a Box2D world object to simulate physics interactions. Define parameters such as gravity, timestep, and iterations for the physics simulation.

Example Code for Initializing Box2D World:

```
b2Vec2 gravity(0.0f, -9.81f); // Define gravity
b2World world(gravity); // Create Box2D world
```

Define Game Objects as Box2D Bodies:

Map game objects to Box2D bodies, which represent physical entities in the simulation. Set properties such as shape, density, friction, and restitution for each body.

Example Code for Creating Box2D Bodies:

```
b2BodyDef bodyDef;
bodyDef.type = b2_dynamicBody; // Define body as dynamic
(affected by physics)
bodyDef.position.Set(x, y); // Set initial position
b2Body* body = world.CreateBody(&bodyDef); // Create body in
Box2D world
b2PolygonShape shape;
shape.SetAsBox(width / 2.0f, height / 2.0f); // Define shape as
rectangle
b2FixtureDef fixtureDef;
fixtureDef.shape = &shape;
fixtureDef.density = 1.0f; // Set density
fixtureDef.friction = 0.3f; // Set friction
fixtureDef.restitution = 0.5f; // Set restitution
body->CreateFixture(&fixtureDef); // Attach fixture to body
```

Simulate Physics Interactions:

Update the Box2D world each frame to simulate physics interactions. Step the simulation forward by a fixed timestep to calculate new positions and velocities of objects.

Example Code for Simulating Physics Interactions:

```cpp
float32 timeStep = 1.0f / 60.0f; // Fixed timestep
int32 velocityIterations = 6; // Iterations for velocity
resolution
int32 positionIterations = 2; // Iterations for position
resolution
world.Step(timeStep, velocityIterations, positionIterations); //
Step physics simulation forward
```

Handle Collision Events:

Implement collision callbacks to detect and respond to collisions between Box2D bodies. Handle collision events by applying forces, triggering game events, or destroying objects.

Example Code for Handling Collision Events:

```cpp
void BeginContact(b2Contact* contact) {
    // Handle collision begin event
}

void EndContact(b2Contact* contact) {
    // Handle collision end event
}
```

By following these steps and incorporating the provided code examples, developers can seamlessly integrate a physics engine like Box2D into their game projects, enabling realistic physics simulations and interactions in the game world.

Audio and Sound Effects

Audio and sound effects play a vital role in enhancing the immersive experience of a game, adding depth, atmosphere, and emotional resonance to the gameplay. In C++ game development, integrating audio features involves utilizing libraries and frameworks to handle sound playback, mixing, and manipulation. By incorporating audio elements effectively, developers can create dynamic and engaging experiences that captivate players' senses and contribute to the overall enjoyment of the game.

One of the primary tasks in implementing audio in C++ games is to select a suitable audio library or API that meets the requirements of the game project. Popular choices include OpenAL, SDL Mixer, and FMOD, each offering a range of features for handling sound effects, music playback, and spatial audio. Once a library is chosen, developers can leverage its functionalities to load and play audio files, adjust volume levels, apply effects, and manage audio resources efficiently.

Spatial audio is a crucial aspect of audio design in games, enabling realistic sound propagation and positioning within the game environment. By utilizing spatial audio techniques, developers can simulate the perception of sound sources originating from specific locations in the game world, creating a sense of depth and immersion for players. Techniques such as 3D audio positioning, distance attenuation, and environmental effects contribute to the spatial realism of soundscapes in games, enhancing the overall audio experience.

In addition to sound effects, music also plays a significant role in setting the mood, pacing, and emotional tone of a game. Integrating dynamic music systems that adapt to gameplay events and player actions can further enhance the interactive experience. By incorporating music seamlessly into the gameplay loop and synchronizing it with in-game events, developers can evoke emotions, build tension, and reinforce the narrative elements of the game, creating a cohesive and memorable audiovisual experience for players. Overall, audio and sound effects are integral components of C++ game development, contributing to the holistic design and immersive quality of modern video games.

Introduction to Game Audio

Game audio refers to the sound elements integrated into video games to enhance the overall gaming experience. It encompasses various components such as sound effects, music, voice acting, and ambient sounds, all of which contribute to the immersive audio landscape of a game.

Importance of Audio in Games:

Audio plays a crucial role in enhancing immersion, atmosphere, and emotional engagement in video games. It complements visual elements by providing auditory cues and feedback, enriching the player's sensory experience.

Well-designed audio can complement gameplay mechanics, reinforce narrative elements, and evoke specific moods or emotions. From the crunch of footsteps to the epic orchestral score, audio elements contribute to the overall ambiance and tone of a game.

Integration of Audio Libraries:

C++ game developers typically integrate audio libraries or APIs to handle sound playback and manipulation. Libraries such as OpenAL, SDL Mixer, and

FMOD offer features for loading audio files, managing sound resources, and implementing spatial audio effects.

Integration involves initializing the audio system, loading audio assets, and controlling playback through code. Developers leverage these libraries to create dynamic and immersive audio experiences within their games.

Spatial Audio and 3D Sound:

Spatial audio techniques simulate the perception of sound sources originating from specific locations within the game world. By implementing 3D sound positioning, developers can create a sense of depth and immersion for players.

Techniques such as distance attenuation, doppler effect, and environmental reverberation contribute to the spatial realism of soundscapes in games. Spatial audio enhances realism, improves player orientation, and adds depth to the game environment.

Dynamic Music Systems:

Dynamic music systems adapt the game's music to match gameplay events, player actions, and narrative progression. Interactive music systems seam-lessly transition between different musical tracks, intensify during action sequences, and relax during exploration or downtime.

- Implementing dynamic music enhances player engagement, reinforces game pacing, and contributes to a cohesive audiovisual experience. By integrating dynamic music systems, developers can create personalized and immersive soundtracks that enhance the overall gaming experience.

Implementing Sound Effects in C++

Implementing sound effects in C++ involves using audio libraries or APIs to load and play audio files, control volume levels, and manage sound resources. Below, I'll provide a basic example of how to implement sound effects using the SDL Mixer library.

Setup SDL Mixer:

- Before using SDL Mixer, make sure to initialize SDL and Mixer subsystems in your application.

Example Code for Initializing SDL Mixer:

```cpp
#include <SDL.h>
#include <SDL_mixer.h>

int main() {
    // Initialize SDL
    if (SDL_Init(SDL_INIT_AUDIO) < 0) {
        // Handle initialization error
        return -1;
    }

    // Initialize SDL Mixer
    if (Mix_OpenAudio(44100, MIX_DEFAULT_FORMAT, 2, 2048) < 0) {
        // Handle initialization error
        return -1;
    }

    // Your game code here

    // Clean up SDL Mixer
    Mix_Quit();

    // Clean up SDL
    SDL_Quit();
```

```
    return 0;
}
```

Load Sound Effects:

- Load sound effect files into memory using SDL Mixer's functions. Sound effects can be in various formats such as WAV or MP3.

Example Code for Loading Sound Effects:

```
// Load sound effect
Mix_Chunk* soundEffect = Mix_LoadWAV("sound_effect.wav");
if (soundEffect == nullptr) {
    // Handle loading error
}
```

Play Sound Effects:

- Play loaded sound effects at desired times or in response to specific game events using SDL Mixer's playback functions.

Example Code for Playing Sound Effects:

```
// Play sound effect
Mix_PlayChannel(-1, soundEffect, 0); // -1 for any available
channel, 0 for no loop
```

Control Sound Effects:

- Adjust volume levels, panning, and other parameters of sound effects using SDL Mixer's control functions.

Example Code for Controlling Sound Effects:

```
// Set volume of sound effect
Mix_VolumeChunk(soundEffect, MIX_MAX_VOLUME / 2); // Half volume

// Set panning of sound effect (left to right, -128 to 127)
Mix_SetPanning(channel, -128, 127);
```

By following these steps and incorporating the provided code examples, developers can effectively implement sound effects in their C++ games using SDL Mixer or other audio libraries, enhancing the overall audio experience for players.

Managing Audio Assets and Mixing

Managing audio assets and mixing involves loading, organizing, and playing audio files, as well as adjusting their volume levels and mixing multiple sounds together. Let's dive into how you can achieve this in C++ using the SDL Mixer library, along with explanations where necessary:

Loading Audio Assets:

Load audio files into memory using SDL Mixer's functions. These files can be sound effects, music tracks, or any other audio resources.

Example Code for Loading Audio Assets:

```
Mix_Chunk* soundEffect = Mix_LoadWAV("sound_effect.wav");
if (soundEffect == nullptr) {
    // Handle loading error
}

Mix_Music* backgroundMusic = Mix_LoadMUS("background_music.mp3");
if (backgroundMusic == nullptr) {
```

```
    // Handle loading error
  }
```

Playing Audio:

Play loaded audio files at desired times or in response to specific game events using SDL Mixer's playback functions.

Example Code for Playing Audio:

```
// Play sound effect
Mix_PlayChannel(-1, soundEffect, 0); // -1 for any available
channel, 0 for no loop

// Play background music
Mix_PlayMusic(backgroundMusic, -1); // -1 for loop indefinitely
```

Adjusting Volume:

Control the volume levels of individual audio assets or the overall volume of the audio output using SDL Mixer's volume control functions.

Example Code for Adjusting Volume:

```
// Set volume of sound effect
Mix_VolumeChunk(soundEffect, MIX_MAX_VOLUME / 2); // Half volume

// Set volume of music
Mix_VolumeMusic(MIX_MAX_VOLUME / 2); // Half volume
```

Mixing Audio:

Mix multiple sounds together by playing them simultaneously on different audio channels. SDL Mixer handles the mixing process automatically.

Example Code for Mixing Audio:

```
// Play multiple sound effects simultaneously
Mix_PlayChannel(-1, soundEffect1, 0);
Mix_PlayChannel(-1, soundEffect2, 0);
```

Unloading Audio Assets:

Release memory allocated for audio assets when they are no longer needed to prevent memory leaks.

Example Code for Unloading Audio Assets:

```
Mix_FreeChunk(soundEffect);
Mix_FreeMusic(backgroundMusic);
```

By following these steps and incorporating the provided code examples, developers can effectively manage audio assets and mixing in their C++ games using SDL Mixer or similar audio libraries. This allows for dynamic audio experiences that enhance the overall immersion and enjoyment of the game.

User Input and Controls

User input and controls are essential aspects of game development, allowing players to interact with and control the game environment. In C++ game development, managing user input involves capturing input events from devices such as keyboards, mice, gamepads, and touchscreens, and translating them into game actions. By handling user input effectively, developers can create responsive and intuitive control schemes that enhance the gameplay experience.

C++ game developers typically use input handling libraries or frameworks such as SDL (Simple DirectMedia Layer) or SFML (Simple and Fast Multimedia Library) to manage user input. These libraries provide functions to detect key presses, mouse movements, joystick inputs, and touch gestures, allowing developers to implement custom control schemes tailored to their games. By capturing and processing input events in real-time, developers can create dynamic and engaging gameplay experiences that respond to player actions with precision and accuracy.

In addition to basic input detection, C++ game developers often implement input buffering, input mapping, and input smoothing techniques to improve the responsiveness and usability of their games. Input buffering ensures that input commands are processed even if they occur between frames, preventing input lag and delays. Input mapping allows players to customize control bindings according to their preferences, accommodating different playstyles and input devices. Input smoothing techniques help to eliminate jitter and improve the consistency of player movements, providing a smoother and more enjoyable gaming experience overall. By mastering the art of user input and controls, developers can create games that are not only technically proficient but also immersive and enjoyable to play.

Handling Keyboard and Mouse Input

Handling keyboard and mouse input is fundamental in game development as it allows players to interact with the game environment. In C++, this is often accomplished using libraries such as SDL or SFML. Below is an example using SDL to handle keyboard and mouse input:

```cpp
#include <SDL.h>

int main() {
    // Initialize SDL
    if (SDL_Init(SDL_INIT_VIDEO) != 0) {
        SDL_Log("Unable to initialize SDL: %s", SDL_GetError());
        return 1;
    }

    // Create a window
    SDL_Window* window = SDL_CreateWindow("Keyboard and Mouse
    Input",
                                          SDL_WINDOWPOS_CENTERED,
                                          SDL_WINDOWPOS_CENTERED,
                                          800, 600,
                                          0);
    if (window == nullptr) {
        SDL_Log("Failed to create window: %s", SDL_GetError());
        return 1;
    }

    // Create a renderer
    SDL_Renderer* renderer = SDL_CreateRenderer(window, -1,
    SDL_RENDERER_ACCELERATED);
    if (renderer == nullptr) {
```

```c
        SDL_Log("Failed to create renderer: %s", SDL_GetError());
        return 1;
    }

// Main loop
bool quit = false;
while (!quit) {
    // Event handling
    SDL_Event event;
    while (SDL_PollEvent(&event)) {
        switch (event.type) {
            case SDL_QUIT:
                quit = true;
                break;
            case SDL_KEYDOWN:
                // Handle key presses
                switch (event.key.keysym.sym) {
                    case SDLK_UP:
                        SDL_Log("Up arrow key pressed");
                        break;
                    case SDLK_DOWN:
                        SDL_Log("Down arrow key pressed");
                        break;
                    case SDLK_LEFT:
                        SDL_Log("Left arrow key pressed");
                        break;
                    case SDLK_RIGHT:
                        SDL_Log("Right arrow key pressed");
                        break;
                    default:
                        break;
                }
                break;
            case SDL_MOUSEBUTTONDOWN:
                // Handle mouse button clicks
                if (event.button.button == SDL_BUTTON_LEFT) {
                    SDL_Log("Left mouse button clicked at
                    (%d, %d)", event.button.x,
                    event.button.y);
                }
```

```
                break;
            default:
                break;
        }
    }

    // Render something to visualize input handling (not
    shown here)

    // Delay to avoid consuming too much CPU
    SDL_Delay(16);
    }

    // Clean up
    SDL_DestroyRenderer(renderer);
    SDL_DestroyWindow(window);
    SDL_Quit();

    return 0;
}
```

Explanation:

- The code initializes SDL and creates a window and a renderer for rendering graphics.
- Inside the main loop, the code continuously polls for SDL events using **SDL_PollEvent**.
- When a **SDL_QUIT** event is detected (e.g., the user closes the window), the program sets **quit** to true, exiting the loop.
- Key presses are handled inside the **SDL_KEYDOWN** case, where **event.key.keysym.sym** represents the pressed key.
- Mouse button clicks are handled inside the **SDL_MOUSEBUTTONDOWN** case, with **event.button.button** representing the pressed mouse button and **event.button.x** and **event.button.y** representing the mouse coordinates.
- Finally, the program cleans up SDL resources before exiting.

This code provides a basic framework for handling keyboard and mouse input in a C++ SDL application. Developers can expand upon this by adding more sophisticated input handling logic and integrating it with game mechanics and rendering.

Implementing Gamepad Support

Implementing gamepad support in a C++ game can greatly enhance the player experience by allowing them to use game controllers for input. SDL (Simple DirectMedia Layer) is a popular library for handling gamepad input in C++. Below is an example of how to implement gamepad support using SDL:

```cpp
#include <SDL.h>

int main() {
    // Initialize SDL
    if (SDL_Init(SDL_INIT_VIDEO | SDL_INIT_GAMECONTROLLER) != 0) {
        SDL_Log("Unable to initialize SDL: %s", SDL_GetError());
        return 1;
    }

    // Check for connected game controllers
    int numControllers = SDL_NumJoysticks();
    if (numControllers < 1) {
        SDL_Log("No game controllers detected");
        return 1;
    }

    // Open the first available game controller
    SDL_GameController* controller = nullptr;
    for (int i = 0; i < numControllers; ++i) {
        if (SDL_IsGameController(i)) {
            controller = SDL_GameControllerOpen(i);
            if (controller) {
                SDL_Log("Game controller connected: %s",
                SDL_GameControllerName(controller));
                break;
```

```cpp
        }
    }
}

if (!controller) {
    SDL_Log("Failed to open game controller: %s",
    SDL_GetError());
    return 1;
}

// Main loop
bool quit = false;
while (!quit) {
    // Event handling
    SDL_Event event;
    while (SDL_PollEvent(&event)) {
        switch (event.type) {
            case SDL_QUIT:
                quit = true;
                break;
            case SDL_CONTROLLERBUTTONDOWN:
                // Handle controller button presses
                SDL_Log("Button %d pressed",
                event.cbutton.button);
                break;
            case SDL_CONTROLLERBUTTONUP:
                // Handle controller button releases
                SDL_Log("Button %d released",
                event.cbutton.button);
                break;
            case SDL_CONTROLLERAXISMOTION:
                // Handle controller axis motion (e.g.,
                joystick movement)
                SDL_Log("Axis %d moved: %d",
                event.caxis.axis, event.caxis.value);
                break;
            default:
                break;
        }
    }
```

```cpp
        // Delay to avoid consuming too much CPU
        SDL_Delay(16);
    }


    // Clean up
    SDL_GameControllerClose(controller);
    SDL_Quit();

    return 0;
}
```

Explanation:

- The code initializes SDL with both video and game controller subsystems enabled.
- It checks for connected game controllers using **SDL_NumJoysticks** and opens the first available controller using **SDL_GameControllerOpen**.
- Inside the main loop, the code continuously polls for SDL events using **SDL_PollEvent**.
- When a game controller button is pressed (**SDL_CONTROLLERBUTTONDOWN**) or released (**SDL_CONTROLLERBUTTONUP**), the program logs the event.
- Similarly, when a controller axis is moved (**SDL_CONTROLLERAXISMOTION**), the program logs the event.
- The main loop continues until the user closes the window (**SDL_QUIT** event).
- Finally, the program cleans up by closing the game controller and quitting SDL.

This code provides a basic framework for implementing gamepad support in a C++ game using SDL. Developers can expand upon this by adding more sophisticated input handling logic and integrating it with game mechanics and rendering.

Touchscreen and Mobile Input Integration

Integrating touchscreen and mobile input in a C++ game is crucial for developing mobile games that provide a seamless and intuitive user experience. SDL (Simple DirectMedia Layer) is a popular library that supports touchscreen input in C++. Below is an example of how to integrate touchscreen input using SDL:

```cpp
#include <SDL.h>

int main() {
    // Initialize SDL
    if (SDL_Init(SDL_INIT_VIDEO | SDL_INIT_EVENTS) != 0) {
        SDL_Log("Unable to initialize SDL: %s", SDL_GetError());
        return 1;
    }

    // Create a window
    SDL_Window* window = SDL_CreateWindow("Touchscreen Input",
                                          SDL_WINDOWPOS_CENTERED,
                                          SDL_WINDOWPOS_CENTERED,
                                          800, 600,
                                          SDL_WINDOW_SHOWN |
                                          SDL_WINDOW_RESIZABLE);
    if (window == nullptr) {
        SDL_Log("Failed to create window: %s", SDL_GetError());
        return 1;
    }

    // Main loop
    bool quit = false;
    while (!quit) {
        // Event handling
        SDL_Event event;
        while (SDL_PollEvent(&event)) {
            switch (event.type) {
                case SDL_QUIT:
                    quit = true;
```

```c
                break;
            case SDL_FINGERDOWN:
                // Handle finger touch
                SDL_Log("Finger down at (%f, %f)",
                event.tfinger.x, event.tfinger.y);
                break;
            case SDL_FINGERUP:
                // Handle finger release
                SDL_Log("Finger up at (%f, %f)",
                event.tfinger.x, event.tfinger.y);
                break;
            case SDL_FINGERMOTION:
                // Handle finger motion
                SDL_Log("Finger moved to (%f, %f)",
                event.tfinger.x, event.tfinger.y);
                break;
            default:
                break;
        }
    }

    // Delay to avoid consuming too much CPU
    SDL_Delay(16);
    }

    // Clean up
    SDL_DestroyWindow(window);
    SDL_Quit();

    return 0;
}
```

Explanation:

- The code initializes SDL with both video and events subsystems enabled.
- It creates a window using SDL_CreateWindow.
- Inside the main loop, the code continuously polls for SDL events using SDL_PollEvent.
- When a finger touches the touchscreen (SDL_FINGERDOWN), the pro-

gram logs the touch event's coordinates.

- Similarly, when a finger is lifted (SDL_FINGERUP) or moved (SDL_FIN-GERMOTION), the program logs the corresponding events.
- The main loop continues until the user closes the window (SDL_QUIT event).
- Finally, the program cleans up by destroying the window and quitting SDL.

This code provides a basic framework for integrating touchscreen input in a C++ game using SDL. Developers can expand upon this by adding more sophisticated input handling logic and integrating it with game mechanics and rendering.

Game AI and Pathfinding

Game AI and pathfinding are essential components of modern video games, contributing to the overall player experience and immersion. Game AI refers to the intelligence exhibited by non-player characters (NPCs) or entities within a game, enabling them to make decisions, interact with the environment, and respond to player actions in a realistic and challenging manner. Pathfinding, on the other hand, focuses on finding the most efficient path from one point to another within the game world, considering obstacles, terrain, and other dynamic factors.

One of the primary objectives of game AI is to create believable and engaging NPC behavior that enhances the game's narrative and gameplay mechanics. Whether it's controlling enemy behavior in combat scenarios, managing non-playable characters in a virtual world, or simulating the behavior of wildlife in open-world games, effective AI algorithms contribute to the overall immersion and replayability of the game. Game developers utilize various AI techniques, including rule-based systems, finite state machines, neural networks, and machine learning algorithms, to create diverse and adaptive AI behaviors tailored to different game genres and scenarios.

Pathfinding algorithms play a crucial role in enabling NPCs and entities to navigate complex game environments efficiently. From guiding characters through mazes and dungeons to directing units in real-time strategy games or optimizing routes for vehicles in racing games, pathfinding algorithms ensure smooth and realistic movement within the game world. Popular pathfinding algorithms such as A* (A-star), Dijkstra's algorithm, and hierarchical pathfinding provide efficient solutions to the problem of finding optimal paths while considering factors such as terrain cost, dynamic obstacles, and path visibility.

Game AI and pathfinding are integral components of game development, shaping the behavior of NPCs and entities and facilitating efficient navigation within the game world. By leveraging advanced AI techniques and pathfinding algorithms, game developers can create immersive and challenging gameplay experiences that captivate players and keep them engaged for hours on end. As technology continues to advance, the evolution of game AI and pathfinding will undoubtedly play a significant role in shaping the future of interactive entertainment.

Introduction to Artificial Intelligence in Games

Artificial Intelligence (AI) in C++ games involves implementing algorithms and techniques to simulate intelligent behavior in non-player characters (NPCs) and entities within the game world. AI adds depth, challenge, and immersion to games by enabling NPCs to make decisions, solve problems, and interact with the player and environment in a believable and dynamic manner. In this introduction, we'll explore various AI techniques commonly used in C++ game development, along with example code and explanations where applicable.

Finite State Machines (FSMs): Finite state machines are a fundamental AI technique used to model NPC behavior by defining a set of states and transitions between them based on certain conditions or events. Each state represents a specific behavior or action that the NPC can perform, such as "idle," "patrol," "attack," or "flee." Transitions between states are triggered by events or conditions, allowing NPCs to react dynamically to changes in the game environment or player actions.

Example Code for Finite State Machine:

```cpp
enum class State { Idle, Patrol, Chase, Attack, Flee };

class NPC {
public:
    State currentState = State::Idle;

    void Update() {
        switch (currentState) {
            case State::Idle:
                // Perform idle behavior
                break;
            case State::Patrol:
                // Perform patrol behavior
                break;
            case State::Chase:
                // Perform chase behavior
                break;
            case State::Attack:
                // Perform attack behavior
                break;
            case State::Flee:
                // Perform flee behavior
                break;
        }
    }
};
```

Decision Trees: Decision trees are hierarchical structures used to model decision-making processes based on a series of logical conditions or criteria. In game AI, decision trees can be used to determine NPC behavior by evaluating various factors such as player proximity, health status, and environmental conditions. Each node in the tree represents a decision point, with branches corresponding to possible actions or outcomes based on the evaluated conditions.

Example Code for Decision Tree:

```cpp
class DecisionTree {
public:
    bool Evaluate(Player player, NPC npc) {
        if (player.IsVisibleToNPC(npc)) {
            if (player.IsInRangeOfNPC(npc)) {
                return npc.AttackPlayer();
            } else {
                return npc.ChasePlayer();
            }
        } else {
            return npc.Patrol();
        }
    }
};
```

Pathfinding Algorithms: Pathfinding algorithms such as A* (A-star) and Dijkstra's algorithm are used to calculate the most efficient path from one point to another within the game world, taking into account obstacles, terrain, and other dynamic factors. NPCs can utilize pathfinding algorithms to navigate complex environments, avoid obstacles, and pursue or evade targets.

Example Code for Pathfinding (using A algorithm):*

```cpp
class Pathfinder {
public:
    std::vector<Node> FindPath(Node start, Node goal) {
        // Implement A* algorithm to find the path
    }
};
```

By leveraging these AI techniques and algorithms, game developers can create dynamic and engaging gameplay experiences that challenge players and immerse them in rich and lifelike virtual worlds. As technology continues to advance, the potential for AI in C++ games to evolve and innovate is limitless, opening up new possibilities for interactive entertainment.

Implementing Basic AI Behaviors

Implementing basic AI behaviors involves creating simple yet effective algorithms to simulate intelligent actions and reactions for non-player characters (NPCs) in a game. Below, I'll provide example code for common AI behaviors such as patrolling, chasing, and attacking, along with explanations where necessary.

Patrolling Behavior:

- Patrolling behavior involves NPCs moving along predefined routes or waypoints within the game world.

Example Code for Patrolling Behavior:

```
class NPC {
private:
    std::vector<Vector2> patrolRoute;
    int currentWaypointIndex = 0;

public:
    void Update() {
        if (patrolRoute.empty()) {
            return; // No patrol route defined
        }

        // Move towards the current waypoint
        Vector2 targetPosition =
        patrolRoute[currentWaypointIndex];
        MoveTowards(targetPosition);

        // Check if reached the current waypoint
        if (DistanceTo(targetPosition) < 1.0f) {
            currentWaypointIndex = (currentWaypointIndex + 1) %
```

```
            patrolRoute.size();
        }
    }
};
```

Explanation:

- The **NPC** class maintains a list of patrol waypoints (**patrolRoute**) and an index to track the current waypoint (**currentWaypointIndex**).
- In the **Update** method, the NPC moves towards the current waypoint and checks if it has reached the waypoint. If reached, it updates the current waypoint index to move to the next waypoint in the patrol route.

Chasing Behavior:

- Chasing behavior involves NPCs pursuing a target, typically the player character, within the game world.

Example Code for Chasing Behavior:

```
class NPC {
private:
    Player* target;

public:
    void Update() {
        if (target == nullptr) {
            return; // No target to chase
        }

        // Move towards the target
        Vector2 targetPosition = target->GetPosition();
        MoveTowards(targetPosition);
    }
};
```

Explanation:

- The **NPC** class contains a pointer to the target (e.g., the player character).
- In the **Update** method, the NPC moves towards the target's position to chase it.

Attacking Behavior:

- Attacking behavior involves NPCs engaging in combat with the target, typically using melee or ranged attacks.

Example Code for Attacking Behavior:

```cpp
class NPC {
private:
    Player* target;
    float attackRange;

public:
    void Update() {
        if (target == nullptr) {
            return; // No target to attack
        }

        float distanceToTarget =
        DistanceTo(target->GetPosition());
        if (distanceToTarget <= attackRange) {
            // Perform attack action
            Attack(target);
        }
    }
};
```

Explanation:

- The **NPC** class contains a pointer to the target (e.g., the player character) and the attack range.

- In the **Update** method, the NPC checks if the target is within the attack range. If so, it performs the attack action.

By implementing these basic AI behaviors, developers can create NPCs that exhibit lifelike actions and reactions, enhancing the overall gameplay experience for players. These behaviors can be further expanded and refined to suit the specific requirements and dynamics of the game.

Pathfinding Algorithms for Game Characters

Pathfinding algorithms are essential in game development for enabling characters to navigate complex environments efficiently. These algorithms calculate the optimal path from a starting point to a destination while avoiding obstacles and considering various factors such as terrain cost, dynamic changes in the environment, and the character's movement capabilities. In this explanation, we'll explore the key concepts of pathfinding algorithms and provide examples where necessary.

A (A-star) Algorithm:*

The A* algorithm is one of the most commonly used pathfinding algorithms in game development due to its efficiency and accuracy. It combines the benefits of both breadth-first search and heuristic search to find the shortest path from the starting point to the goal.

Example of A Algorithm:*

```cpp
class AStar {
public:
    std::vector<Node> FindPath(Node start, Node goal) {
        std::priority_queue<Node, std::vector<Node>,
        CompareNodes> openSet;
        std::unordered_set<Node> closedSet;
```

```cpp
        start.gScore = 0;
        start.fScore = Heuristic(start, goal);
        openSet.push(start);

        while (!openSet.empty()) {
            Node current = openSet.top();
            openSet.pop();

            if (current == goal) {
                return ReconstructPath(current);
            }

            closedSet.insert(current);

            for (Node neighbor : GetNeighbors(current)) {
                if (closedSet.find(neighbor) != closedSet.end()) {
                    continue; // Skip already evaluated nodes
                }

                float tentativeGScore = current.gScore +
                Distance(current, neighbor);

                if (tentativeGScore < neighbor.gScore) {
                    neighbor.cameFrom = current;
                    neighbor.gScore = tentativeGScore;
                    neighbor.fScore = neighbor.gScore +
                    Heuristic(neighbor, goal);

                    if (std::find(openSet.begin(), openSet.end(),
                    neighbor) == openSet.end()) {
                        openSet.push(neighbor);
                    }
                }
            }
        }

        return std::vector<Node>(); // No path found
    }
};
```

Explanation:

- The A* algorithm maintains two sets: an open set of nodes to be evaluated and a closed set of nodes that have already been evaluated.
- It starts by initializing the starting node's scores and adding it to the open set.
- The algorithm iterates through the open set, evaluating neighboring nodes and updating their scores if a shorter path is found.
- It uses a heuristic function to estimate the cost of reaching the goal from each node.
- The algorithm continues until the goal is reached or the open set is empty.

Dijkstra's Algorithm:

Dijkstra's algorithm is another popular pathfinding algorithm that finds the shortest path from a starting point to all other reachable nodes in a graph. Unlike A*, it does not use a heuristic function and explores nodes in order of their distance from the starting point.

Example of Dijkstra's Algorithm:

```cpp
class Dijkstra {
public:
    std::vector<Node> FindShortestPath(Node start) {
        std::priority_queue<Node, std::vector<Node>,
        CompareNodes> openSet;
        start.distance = 0;
        openSet.push(start);

        while (!openSet.empty()) {
            Node current = openSet.top();
            openSet.pop();

            for (Node neighbor : GetNeighbors(current)) {
                float tentativeDistance = current.distance +
```

```
            Distance(current, neighbor);
            if (tentativeDistance < neighbor.distance) {
                neighbor.distance = tentativeDistance;
                neighbor.cameFrom = current;
                openSet.push(neighbor);
            }
        }
    }

    return ReconstructPath(start);
  }
};
```

Explanation:

- Dijkstra's algorithm maintains a priority queue of nodes to be evaluated, prioritized by their distance from the starting point.
- It starts by initializing the starting node's distance and adding it to the priority queue.
- The algorithm iterates through the priority queue, evaluating neighboring nodes and updating their distances if a shorter path is found.
- It continues until all reachable nodes have been evaluated.

By utilizing pathfinding algorithms like A* and Dijkstra's algorithm, game developers can create intelligent characters that navigate the game world efficiently, enhancing the overall player experience. These algorithms can be further optimized and customized to suit the specific requirements of different game genres and environments.

Networking and Multiplayer

Networking and multiplayer functionality play pivotal roles in modern game development, fostering social interaction and expanding the player experience beyond single-player modes. Networking allows games to connect players across different devices and locations, enabling collaborative gameplay, competitive matches, and shared experiences. Multiplayer games leverage networking technology to facilitate real-time communication between players, synchronize game state across multiple devices, and handle complex interactions between participants.

Implementing networking and multiplayer functionality involves several key components, including client-server architecture, peer-to-peer networking, and network protocols such as TCP/IP and UDP. In client-server architecture, one device (the server) manages game state and coordinates interactions between multiple clients, while peer-to-peer networking enables direct communication between individual devices without a central server. Developers must also consider latency, bandwidth limitations, and network stability when designing and implementing multiplayer features to ensure smooth and responsive gameplay experiences for all participants.

Overall, networking and multiplayer capabilities enrich gaming experiences by fostering community engagement, enabling cooperative gameplay, and enhancing competitive interactions. With advancements in networking technology and online infrastructure, multiplayer gaming continues to evolve, offering players new opportunities for social interaction, collaboration, and competition in virtual worlds. As game developers harness the power of networking, multiplayer gaming will remain a cornerstone of the gaming industry, connecting players worldwide and shaping the future of interactive entertainment.

Introduction to Network Programming

Introduction to network programming in C++ gaming involves understanding how to establish connections between game clients and servers, exchange data over the network, and synchronize game state across multiple devices. This typically involves using socket programming to create network communication channels and implementing protocols for data transmission. Below, I'll provide an example of a simple client–server architecture in C++ for gaming, along with explanations where possible.

Server Side:

- The server manages game state, receives input from clients, processes game logic, and sends updates to all connected clients.

```cpp
#include <iostream>
#include <string>
#include <WS2tcpip.h> // Windows Socket API

#pragma comment(lib, "ws2_32.lib") // Link Windows Socket library

int main() {
    // Initialize Winsock
    WSADATA wsData;
    WORD ver = MAKEWORD(2, 2);
    int wsOK = WSAStartup(ver, &wsData);
    if (wsOK != 0) {
        std::cerr << "Can't initialize Winsock! Quitting" <<
        std::endl;
```

```cpp
        return -1;
    }

    // Create a socket
    SOCKET serverSocket = socket(AF_INET, SOCK_STREAM, 0);
    if (serverSocket == INVALID_SOCKET) {
        std::cerr << "Can't create server socket! Quitting" <<
        std::endl;
        return -1;
    }

    // Bind the socket to an IP address and port
    sockaddr_in hint;
    hint.sin_family = AF_INET;
    hint.sin_port = htons(54000);
    hint.sin_addr.S_un.S_addr = INADDR_ANY; // Bind to any
    available address

    bind(serverSocket, (sockaddr*)&hint, sizeof(hint));

    // Tell Winsock the socket is for listening
    listen(serverSocket, SOMAXCONN);

    // Wait for a connection
    sockaddr_in client;
    int clientSize = sizeof(client);
    SOCKET clientSocket = accept(serverSocket,
    (sockaddr*)&client, &clientSize);
    if (clientSocket == INVALID_SOCKET) {
        std::cerr << "Can't accept client connection! Quitting"
        << std::endl;
        return -1;
    }

    // Close server socket when done
    closesocket(serverSocket);

    // Receive and send data
    char buf[4096];
    while (true) {
```

```cpp
        ZeroMemory(buf, 4096);
        int bytesReceived = recv(clientSocket, buf, 4096, 0);
        if (bytesReceived == SOCKET_ERROR) {
            std::cerr << "Error in recv()! Quitting" << std::endl;
            break;
        }

        if (bytesReceived == 0) {
            std::cout << "Client disconnected" << std::endl;
            break;
        }

        std::cout << "Received: " << std::string(buf, 0,
        bytesReceived) << std::endl;
    }

    // Close client socket
    closesocket(clientSocket);

    // Cleanup Winsock
    WSACleanup();

    return 0;
}
```

Explanation:

- This code sets up a server socket using the Windows Socket API (Winsock).
- It binds the socket to a specific IP address and port.
- The server listens for incoming connections and accepts client connections.
- It receives data from connected clients and prints it to the console.

Client Side:

- The client connects to the server, sends input or commands, receives updates from the server, and renders the game accordingly.

```cpp
#include <iostream>
#include <WS2tcpip.h>

#pragma comment(lib, "ws2_32.lib")

int main() {
    // Initialize Winsock
    WSADATA wsData;
    WORD ver = MAKEWORD(2, 2);
    int wsOK = WSAStartup(ver, &wsData);
    if (wsOK != 0) {
        std::cerr << "Can't initialize Winsock! Quitting" <<
        std::endl;
        return -1;
    }

    // Create a socket
    SOCKET clientSocket = socket(AF_INET, SOCK_STREAM, 0);
    if (clientSocket == INVALID_SOCKET) {
        std::cerr << "Can't create client socket! Quitting" <<
        std::endl;
        return -1;
    }

    // Connect to the server
    sockaddr_in hint;
    hint.sin_family = AF_INET;
    hint.sin_port = htons(54000);
    inet_pton(AF_INET, "127.0.0.1", &hint.sin_addr);

    int connectResult = connect(clientSocket, (sockaddr*)&hint,
    sizeof(hint));
    if (connectResult == SOCKET_ERROR) {
        std::cerr << "Can't connect to server! Quitting" <<
        std::endl;
        closesocket(clientSocket);
        WSACleanup();
        return -1;
```

```cpp
    }

    // Send and receive data
    std::string userInput;
    while (true) {
        std::cout << "> ";
        std::getline(std::cin, userInput);

        if (userInput.size() > 0) {
            int sendResult = send(clientSocket,
            userInput.c_str(), userInput.size() + 1, 0);
            if (sendResult != SOCKET_ERROR) {
                char buf[4096];
                ZeroMemory(buf, 4096);
                int bytesReceived = recv(clientSocket, buf, 4096,
                0);
                if (bytesReceived > 0) {
                    std::cout << "Server: " << std::string(buf,
                    0, bytesReceived) << std::endl;
                }
            }
        }
    }

    // Cleanup Winsock
    closesocket(clientSocket);
    WSACleanup();

    return 0;
}
```

Explanation:

- This code sets up a client socket and connects to the server using Winsock.
- It sends user input to the server and receives data from the server.
- The client can send commands or updates to the server and receive responses or game state updates.

By understanding and implementing networking code like the examples above, game developers can create multiplayer games that allow players to interact and play together over the network, providing a rich and immersive gaming experience.

Implementing Multiplayer Support in C++

Implementing multiplayer support in C++ involves establishing network connections between multiple game clients and a central server, exchanging data between them, and synchronizing game state across all connected clients. Below, I'll provide an example of a simple client-server architecture for a multiplayer game in C++, along with explanations where necessary.

Server Side:

- The server manages game state, receives input from clients, processes game logic, and sends updates to all connected clients.

```cpp
// Server.cpp

#include <iostream>
#include <vector>
#include <WS2tcpip.h> // Windows Socket API

#pragma comment(lib, "ws2_32.lib") // Link Windows Socket library

int main() {
    // Initialize Winsock
    WSADATA wsData;
    WORD ver = MAKEWORD(2, 2);
    int wsOK = WSAStartup(ver, &wsData);
    if (wsOK != 0) {
        std::cerr << "Can't initialize Winsock! Quitting" <<
        std::endl;
        return -1;
    }
```

```cpp
// Create a socket
SOCKET serverSocket = socket(AF_INET, SOCK_STREAM, 0);
if (serverSocket == INVALID_SOCKET) {
    std::cerr << "Can't create server socket! Quitting" <<
    std::endl;
    return -1;
}

// Bind the socket to an IP address and port
sockaddr_in hint;
hint.sin_family = AF_INET;
hint.sin_port = htons(54000);
hint.sin_addr.S_un.S_addr = INADDR_ANY; // Bind to any
available address

bind(serverSocket, (sockaddr*)&hint, sizeof(hint));

// Tell Winsock the socket is for listening
listen(serverSocket, SOMAXCONN);

std::vector<SOCKET> clientSockets;

// Wait for connections
while (true) {
    // Accept a new connection
    sockaddr_in client;
    int clientSize = sizeof(client);
    SOCKET clientSocket = accept(serverSocket,
    (sockaddr*)&client, &clientSize);
    if (clientSocket == INVALID_SOCKET) {
        std::cerr << "Can't accept client connection!
        Quitting" << std::endl;
        break;
    }

    // Add client socket to the vector
    clientSockets.push_back(clientSocket);

    // Handle client input and send updates
```

```cpp
        char buf[4096];
        while (true) {
            ZeroMemory(buf, 4096);

            // Receive client input
            int bytesReceived = recv(clientSocket, buf, 4096, 0);
            if (bytesReceived <= 0) {
                std::cerr << "Client disconnected" << std::endl;
                break;
            }

            // Broadcast received data to all clients
            for (SOCKET& socket : clientSockets) {
                if (socket != clientSocket) {
                    send(socket, buf, bytesReceived, 0);
                }
            }
        }
    }

    // Cleanup Winsock
    closesocket(serverSocket);
    WSACleanup();

    return 0;
}
```

Explanation:

- This code sets up a server socket using the Windows Socket API (Winsock).
- It binds the socket to a specific IP address and port and listens for incoming connections.
- When a client connects, the server accepts the connection and adds the client socket to a vector.
- The server continuously receives input from clients and broadcasts it to all connected clients except the sender.

Client Side:

- The client connects to the server, sends input or commands, receives updates from the server, and renders the game accordingly.

```cpp
// Client.cpp

#include <iostream>
#include <WS2tcpip.h>

#pragma comment(lib, "ws2_32.lib")

int main() {
    // Initialize Winsock
    WSADATA wsData;
    WORD ver = MAKEWORD(2, 2);
    int wsOK = WSAStartup(ver, &wsData);
    if (wsOK != 0) {
        std::cerr << "Can't initialize Winsock! Quitting" <<
        std::endl;
        return -1;
    }

    // Create a socket
    SOCKET clientSocket = socket(AF_INET, SOCK_STREAM, 0);
    if (clientSocket == INVALID_SOCKET) {
        std::cerr << "Can't create client socket! Quitting" <<
        std::endl;
        return -1;
    }

    // Connect to the server
    sockaddr_in hint;
    hint.sin_family = AF_INET;
    hint.sin_port = htons(54000);
    inet_pton(AF_INET, "127.0.0.1", &hint.sin_addr);

    int connectResult = connect(clientSocket, (sockaddr*)&hint,
    sizeof(hint));
    if (connectResult == SOCKET_ERROR) {
```

```cpp
        std::cerr << "Can't connect to server! Quitting" <<
        std::endl;
        closesocket(clientSocket);
        WSACleanup();
        return -1;
    }

    // Send and receive data
    std::string userInput;
    char buf[4096];
    while (true) {
        // Receive data from the server
        ZeroMemory(buf, 4096);
        int bytesReceived = recv(clientSocket, buf, 4096, 0);
        if (bytesReceived > 0) {
            std::cout << "Received: " << std::string(buf, 0,
            bytesReceived) << std::endl;
        }

        // Send user input to the server
        std::cout << "> ";
        std::getline(std::cin, userInput);
        if (!userInput.empty()) {
            send(clientSocket, userInput.c_str(),
            userInput.size() + 1, 0);
        }
    }

    // Cleanup Winsock
    closesocket(clientSocket);
    WSACleanup();

    return 0;
}
```

Explanation:

- This code sets up a client socket and connects to the server using Winsock.
- It continuously receives data from the server and prints it to the console.

- The client sends user input to the server whenever the user enters a message.

By understanding and implementing multiplayer support like the examples above, game developers can create multiplayer games where multiple players can interact and play together over a network, enhancing the overall gaming experience.

Server-Client Architecture for Online Games

Implementing a server-client architecture for online games in C++ involves creating a central server that manages game state, communicates with connected clients, and orchestrates gameplay. Clients connect to the server to participate in the game, send input commands, and receive updates about the game world. Below, I'll provide an in-depth explanation along with code examples for both the server and client sides.

Server Side:

The server side of the architecture manages the game state and coordinates communication between multiple clients. It listens for incoming connections, accepts client connections, processes client input, and broadcasts updates to all connected clients.

```cpp
// Server.cpp

#include <iostream>
#include <vector>
#include <WS2tcpip.h> // Windows Socket API

#pragma comment(lib, "ws2_32.lib") // Link Windows Socket library

int main() {
    // Initialize Winsock
```

```cpp
WSADATA wsData;
WORD ver = MAKEWORD(2, 2);
int wsOK = WSAStartup(ver, &wsData);
if (wsOK != 0) {
    std::cerr << "Can't initialize Winsock! Quitting" <<
    std::endl;
    return -1;
}

// Create a socket
SOCKET serverSocket = socket(AF_INET, SOCK_STREAM, 0);
if (serverSocket == INVALID_SOCKET) {
    std::cerr << "Can't create server socket! Quitting" <<
    std::endl;
    return -1;
}

// Bind the socket to an IP address and port
sockaddr_in hint;
hint.sin_family = AF_INET;
hint.sin_port = htons(54000);
hint.sin_addr.S_un.S_addr = INADDR_ANY; // Bind to any
available address

bind(serverSocket, (sockaddr*)&hint, sizeof(hint));

// Tell Winsock the socket is for listening
listen(serverSocket, SOMAXCONN);

std::vector<SOCKET> clientSockets;

// Wait for connections
while (true) {
    // Accept a new connection
    sockaddr_in client;
    int clientSize = sizeof(client);
    SOCKET clientSocket = accept(serverSocket,
    (sockaddr*)&client, &clientSize);
    if (clientSocket == INVALID_SOCKET) {
        std::cerr << "Can't accept client connection!
```

```cpp
            Quitting" << std::endl;
            break;
        }

        // Add client socket to the vector
        clientSockets.push_back(clientSocket);

        // Handle client input and send updates
        char buf[4096];
        while (true) {
            ZeroMemory(buf, 4096);

            // Receive client input
            int bytesReceived = recv(clientSocket, buf, 4096, 0);
            if (bytesReceived <= 0) {
                std::cerr << "Client disconnected" << std::endl;
                break;
            }

            // Broadcast received data to all clients
            for (SOCKET& socket : clientSockets) {
                if (socket != clientSocket) {
                    send(socket, buf, bytesReceived, 0);
                }
            }
        }
    }

    // Cleanup Winsock
    closesocket(serverSocket);
    WSACleanup();

    return 0;
}
```

Client Side:

The client side connects to the server, sends input commands, and receives
updates about the game world from the server.

```cpp
// Client.cpp

#include <iostream>
#include <WS2tcpip.h>

#pragma comment(lib, "ws2_32.lib")

int main() {
    // Initialize Winsock
    WSADATA wsData;
    WORD ver = MAKEWORD(2, 2);
    int wsOK = WSAStartup(ver, &wsData);
    if (wsOK != 0) {
        std::cerr << "Can't initialize Winsock! Quitting" <<
        std::endl;
        return -1;
    }

    // Create a socket
    SOCKET clientSocket = socket(AF_INET, SOCK_STREAM, 0);
    if (clientSocket == INVALID_SOCKET) {
        std::cerr << "Can't create client socket! Quitting" <<
        std::endl;
        return -1;
    }

    // Connect to the server
    sockaddr_in hint;
    hint.sin_family = AF_INET;
    hint.sin_port = htons(54000);
    inet_pton(AF_INET, "127.0.0.1", &hint.sin_addr);

    int connectResult = connect(clientSocket, (sockaddr*)&hint,
    sizeof(hint));
    if (connectResult == SOCKET_ERROR) {
        std::cerr << "Can't connect to server! Quitting" <<
        std::endl;
        closesocket(clientSocket);
```

```cpp
        WSACleanup();
        return -1;
    }

    // Send and receive data
    std::string userInput;
    char buf[4096];
    while (true) {
        // Receive data from the server
        ZeroMemory(buf, 4096);
        int bytesReceived = recv(clientSocket, buf, 4096, 0);
        if (bytesReceived > 0) {
            std::cout << "Received: " << std::string(buf, 0,
            bytesReceived) << std::endl;
        }

        // Send user input to the server
        std::cout << "> ";
        std::getline(std::cin, userInput);
        if (!userInput.empty()) {
            send(clientSocket, userInput.c_str(),
            userInput.size() + 1, 0);
        }
    }

    // Cleanup Winsock
    closesocket(clientSocket);
    WSACleanup();

    return 0;
}
```

Explanation:

- The server listens for incoming connections using **'listen'** and accepts new connections using **'accept'**.
- Upon accepting a new connection, the server adds the client socket to a vector of client sockets.
- The server continuously receives input from each client using **'recv'** and

broadcasts it to all connected clients using **'send'**.
- The client connects to the server using **'connect'**, sends user input to the server using **'send'**, and receives updates from the server using **'recv'**.

By implementing this server-client architecture, game developers can create online multiplayer games where multiple players can interact and play together in real-time, enhancing the gaming experience and fostering community engagement.

Optimization Techniques for High-Performance

Optimization techniques for high-performance gaming involve fine-tuning various aspects of game development to ensure smooth and efficient operation, even on resource-constrained devices. These techniques encompass a range of strategies, from optimizing code execution and memory usage to leveraging hardware acceleration and minimizing rendering overhead. By carefully optimizing critical components of the game, developers can achieve better performance, reduce latency, and enhance the overall player experience.

One key aspect of optimization is code optimization, which involves refining algorithms, minimizing redundant operations, and reducing computational complexity to improve execution speed and efficiency. This includes techniques such as loop unrolling, data structure optimization, and algorithmic improvements tailored to specific game mechanics. Additionally, optimizing memory usage is crucial for maximizing performance, as efficient memory management can minimize memory overhead and reduce memory access latency, leading to smoother gameplay and faster loading times.

Furthermore, leveraging hardware acceleration through technologies like graphics processing units (GPUs) and parallel computing can significantly boost performance in graphics-intensive games. Techniques such as shader optimization, texture compression, and parallel processing enable developers to harness the full potential of modern hardware and deliver visually stunning and responsive gaming experiences. By combining these optimization techniques with thorough profiling and testing, developers can create high-performance games that run smoothly across a variety of platforms and devices, maximizing player enjoyment and satisfaction.

Profiling and Performance Analysis

Profiling and performance analysis are essential in C++ game development to identify bottlenecks, optimize code, and improve overall game performance. Profiling tools help developers understand where the application spends the most time and resources, allowing them to prioritize optimization efforts effectively. Below is an example of how to perform basic profiling using the built-in timing functions in C++:

```cpp
#include <iostream>
#include <chrono>

void timeConsumingFunction() {
    // Simulate a time-consuming operation
    for (int i = 0; i < 1000000; ++i) {
        // Some computation
    }
}

int main() {
    // Start timing
    auto startTime = std::chrono::high_resolution_clock::now();

    // Call the function to be profiled
    timeConsumingFunction();

    // Stop timing
    auto endTime = std::chrono::high_resolution_clock::now();

    // Calculate the duration
```

```cpp
    auto duration =
    std::chrono::duration_cast<std::chrono::milliseconds>(endTime
    - startTime);

    // Output the profiling results
    std::cout << "Execution time: " << duration.count() << "
    milliseconds" << std::endl;

    return 0;
}
```

Explanation:

- In this example, we have a **timeConsumingFunction()** that represents a potentially performance-critical part of the game code.
- We use **std::chrono** to measure the execution time of this function by capturing the start and end times with **std::chrono::high_resolution_clock**.
- The **duration** is calculated by subtracting the start time from the end time and converting it to milliseconds.
- Finally, we output the duration to the console to analyze the performance of the function.

While this is a basic example, more sophisticated profiling tools like Intel VTune, AMD CodeXL, or NVIDIA Nsight can provide detailed insights into CPU and GPU usage, memory allocation, and threading behavior. These tools allow developers to identify hotspots in their code and optimize performance effectively. Additionally, integrating profiling into the development workflow ensures that performance considerations are addressed from the outset, leading to faster, more responsive, and more enjoyable gaming experiences.

Memory Management Best Practices

Memory management is crucial in C++ game programming to ensure efficient resource utilization, prevent memory leaks, and optimize performance. Following best practices helps minimize overhead and ensures smooth gameplay. Below are some memory management best practices along with code examples and explanations where necessary:

Use Smart Pointers: Smart pointers, such as **std::unique_ptr** and **std::shared_ptr**, help manage memory automatically by deallocating memory when it's no longer needed. Use **std::unique_ptr** for exclusive ownership and **std::shared_ptr** for shared ownership.

```cpp
#include <memory>

// Example using std::unique_ptr
void exampleFunction() {
    std::unique_ptr<int> ptr = std::make_unique<int>(42);
    // ptr automatically deallocates memory when it goes out of
    scope
}
```

Prefer Stack Allocation: Stack allocation is faster than heap allocation and reduces the likelihood of memory fragmentation. Use stack allocation for small, short-lived objects whenever possible.

```cpp
void exampleFunction() {
    int value = 42; // Stack allocation
}
```

Minimize Dynamic Memory Allocation: Minimize dynamic memory allocation during gameplay to reduce overhead. Preallocate memory for frequently used objects or use object pools to recycle memory.

```cpp
#include <vector>

// Example using std::vector with preallocation
void exampleFunction() {
    std::vector<int> vec;
    vec.reserve(1000); // Preallocate memory for 1000 elements
}
```

Release Resources Timely: Release resources, such as textures, sounds, and shaders, when they're no longer needed to avoid memory leaks and resource exhaustion.

```cpp
// Example releasing texture resources
void unloadTexture(Texture* texture) {
    delete texture;
}
```

Avoid Raw Pointers When Possible: Raw pointers require manual memory management and are prone to errors such as memory leaks and dangling pointers. Prefer smart pointers or container classes like **std::vector** and **std::array**.

```cpp
// Example using std::vector instead of raw pointers
void exampleFunction() {
    std::vector<int> vec(10); // Dynamic array with automatic
    memory management
}
```

By following these memory management best practices, game developers can create more efficient, reliable, and maintainable C++ games while minimizing the risk of memory-related issues. Efficient memory management contributes to better overall performance and enhances the gaming experience for players.

Optimizing Graphics and Rendering Pipeline

Optimizing the graphics and rendering pipeline is essential in game development to achieve high frame rates, smooth animations, and immersive visuals. It involves minimizing rendering overhead, optimizing shaders and textures, and leveraging hardware acceleration effectively. Below, I'll explain several optimization techniques along with code examples where necessary:

Batching and Mesh Optimization: Minimize the number of draw calls by batching together objects with similar properties, such as material and shader. Merge multiple meshes into a single vertex buffer to reduce CPU–GPU communication overhead.

```cpp
// Example of batching objects with similar properties
for (const auto& object : objects) {
    // Bind shader, material, and texture
    object.shader.bind();
    object.material.bind();
    object.texture.bind();

    // Draw the object
    object.mesh.draw();
}
```

Level of Detail (LOD) Optimization: Use lower-detail models for objects that are farther away from the camera to reduce polygon count and improve performance. Implement LOD systems that dynamically adjust the level of detail based on distance and screen size.

```cpp
// Example of LOD optimization
if (distanceToCamera > LOD_threshold) {
    // Render high-detail model
} else {
    // Render low-detail model
}
```

Texture and Shader Optimization: Optimize textures by using texture atlases to reduce texture swaps and minimize memory bandwidth usage. Compress textures to reduce file size and memory footprint. Use shader optimization techniques such as loop unrolling, constant folding, and minimizing texture lookups.

```
// Example of texture atlas usage
TextureAtlas atlas("textures.png");
atlas.setTextureRect(spriteRect);
```

GPU Instancing: Use GPU instancing to render multiple instances of the same object with a single draw call, reducing CPU overhead and improving rendering performance.

```
// Example of GPU instancing
glDrawElementsInstanced(GL_TRIANGLES, numIndices,
GL_UNSIGNED_INT, 0, numInstances);
```

Asynchronous Compute and Multi-Threading: Offload compute-intensive tasks such as physics simulations and AI calculations to separate CPU cores or GPU compute units to parallelize workload and improve performance.

```
// Example of multi-threading using std::async
std::future<void> result = std::async(std::launch::async, [&]() {
    // Perform expensive computation
});
```

Culling and Occlusion Techniques: Implement frustum culling to discard objects outside the view frustum and occlusion culling to skip rendering of occluded objects, reducing unnecessary rendering workload.

```
// Example of frustum culling
if (objectIsInsideFrustum(object)) {
```

```
    // Render the object
}
```

By applying these optimization techniques to the graphics and rendering pipeline, game developers can create visually stunning games that run smoothly across a variety of platforms and hardware configurations, delivering an exceptional gaming experience to players.

Testing, Debugging, and Deployment

Testing, debugging, and deployment are critical phases in C++ game development to ensure the stability, performance, and compatibility of the game across different platforms and environments. During the testing phase, developers conduct various tests, including unit tests, integration tests, and regression tests, to identify and fix bugs, errors, and issues in the game code. Comprehensive testing helps ensure the game functions as intended and meets the quality standards before release.

Debugging plays a vital role in identifying and resolving issues encountered during development and testing. Developers use debugging tools and techniques to track down bugs, analyze runtime behavior, and inspect variables, memory, and call stacks. By pinpointing and fixing bugs early in the development cycle, developers can prevent issues from escalating and ensure the game's stability and performance.

Deployment involves packaging the game for distribution and release to players. Developers optimize game assets, compile the code for target platforms, and package the game files into installers or distribution packages. They also perform compatibility testing on different platforms and devices to ensure the game runs smoothly and meets the requirements of players. A successful deployment process ensures that players can access and enjoy the game without encountering technical issues or compatibility issues, ultimately contributing to a positive gaming experience.

Strategies for Testing Game Code

Testing game code in C++ involves implementing various strategies to ensure the correctness, stability, and performance of the game. Below are some strategies commonly used in C++ game development:

Unit Testing: Unit testing involves testing individual units or components of the game code in isolation to verify their functionality. Developers write test cases for functions, classes, and modules to validate their behavior and edge cases. Unit testing frameworks like Google Test and Catch2 provide tools for automating test execution and reporting results.

Integration Testing: Integration testing verifies the interaction and integration between different modules or systems within the game. Developers test how components interact with each other, including gameplay systems, graphics rendering, audio playback, and input handling. Integration tests ensure that all parts of the game work together seamlessly and produce the desired outcomes.

Regression Testing: Regression testing involves retesting previously developed and tested code to ensure that recent changes or additions haven't introduced new bugs or regressions. Developers rerun existing test cases and compare the results against expected outcomes to detect any discrepancies or unexpected behavior. Regression testing helps maintain code stability and prevents reintroducing fixed issues.

Automated Testing: Automated testing utilizes scripts and tools to automate the execution of test cases, reducing manual effort and increasing testing efficiency. Developers use automation frameworks like Jenkins, Travis CI, or Azure Pipelines to set up continuous integration (CI) and continuous deployment (CD) pipelines. Automated testing ensures that changes to the codebase are thoroughly tested and validated before integration into the main branch.

Performance Testing: Performance testing evaluates the performance characteristics of the game, including frame rate, loading times, memory usage, and CPU/GPU utilization. Developers use profiling tools and performance monitoring software to identify performance bottlenecks and optimize resource usage. Performance testing ensures that the game meets performance requirements and delivers a smooth gaming experience to players.

User Acceptance Testing (UAT): User acceptance testing involves letting actual users or testers play the game and provide feedback on its functionality, usability, and overall experience. Developers collect feedback from testers, analyze reported issues, and prioritize fixes and improvements based on user feedback. UAT helps ensure that the game meets the expectations and preferences of its target audience.

By implementing these testing strategies, C++ game developers can identify and address issues early in the development process, resulting in a more stable, reliable, and enjoyable gaming experience for players.

Debugging Techniques for C++ Games

Debugging C++ games requires a combination of techniques and tools to identify and resolve issues efficiently. Here are some debugging techniques commonly used in C++ game development:

Print Statements: Printing debug information to the console or log files is a straightforward way to inspect the state of variables, objects, and game events during runtime. Developers strategically place print statements throughout the code to track the flow of execution and identify unexpected behavior.

```cpp
void update() {
    // Print debug information
```

```cpp
    std::cout << "Updating game state..." << std::endl;

    // Update game logic
    // ...
}
```

Debugging Tools: Integrated development environments (IDEs) like Visual Studio, Xcode, and CLion offer powerful debugging features, including breakpoints, watchlists, call stacks, and variable inspection. Developers can set breakpoints at specific lines of code to pause execution and examine the program's state, making it easier to identify logic errors and memory issues.

Memory Debugging: Memory-related bugs, such as memory leaks, buffer overflows, and dangling pointers, can cause crashes and instability in C++ games. Memory debugging tools like Valgrind, AddressSanitizer, and Visual Studio's Memory Debugger help detect and diagnose memory-related issues by analyzing memory allocations, accesses, and deallocations.

Profiling Tools: Profiling tools like Intel VTune, AMD CodeXL, and NVIDIA Nsight provide insights into the performance of C++ games by measuring CPU and GPU usage, memory usage, and frame rates. Developers use profiling data to identify performance bottlenecks, optimize critical code paths, and improve overall game performance.

Remote Debugging: Remote debugging allows developers to debug C++ games running on remote devices or platforms, such as consoles or mobile devices. IDEs like Visual Studio and CLion support remote debugging over network connections or USB cables, enabling developers to debug games on target hardware in real-time.

Error Handling and Logging: Implementing robust error handling and logging mechanisms helps capture and report errors and exceptions encountered during runtime. Developers can use logging libraries like spdlog or Boost.Log to log debug information, warnings, errors, and crashes to log files for later analysis.

By leveraging these debugging techniques and tools, C++ game developers can effectively diagnose and resolve issues, ensuring that their games run smoothly and deliver an optimal gaming experience to players.

Deploying Your Game on Multiple Platforms

Deploying a game on multiple platforms involves adapting the game to run on different operating systems, hardware configurations, and distribution platforms while ensuring compatibility, performance, and user experience. Here are the steps to deploy your C++ game on multiple platforms:

- **Platform Compatibility:** Ensure that your game code and dependencies are compatible with the target platforms. This may involve making adjustments for differences in APIs, libraries, and hardware capabilities between platforms. Use platform-agnostic libraries and frameworks where possible to minimize platform-specific code.
- **Cross-Compilation:** Use cross-compilation tools and build systems to generate executable binaries for different target platforms from a single codebase. Set up build configurations and scripts to compile the game code for Windows, macOS, Linux, consoles, and mobile devices using appropriate compilers and toolchains.
- **Testing and Quality Assurance:** Test the game extensively on each target platform to identify and fix platform-specific issues, including performance, graphics rendering, input handling, and compatibility with different hardware configurations. Conduct thorough regression testing to ensure that changes don't introduce new bugs or regressions on any platform.
- **Distribution Platforms:** Choose distribution platforms and storefronts where you want to release your game, such as Steam, Epic Games Store, Apple App Store, Google Play Store, or console storefronts (e.g.,

PlayStation Store, Xbox Live). Follow the guidelines and requirements of each platform for submission, certification, and publishing your game.

- **Packaging and Distribution:** Package your game assets, executable binaries, and dependencies into installers, archives, or distribution packages suitable for each platform. Include platform-specific launchers, icons, metadata, and configuration files as required by distribution platforms and storefronts.

- **Compliance and Certification:** Ensure that your game complies with the policies, guidelines, and technical requirements of each platform and distribution platform. Obtain necessary certifications, ratings, and approvals (e.g., ESRB ratings, PEGI ratings, age ratings) for your game before publishing it on platforms that require them.

- **Marketing and Promotion:** Plan marketing and promotional activities to raise awareness and generate interest in your game across different platforms. Create platform-specific marketing materials, trailers, screenshots, and promotional campaigns tailored to the target audience of each platform.

- **Post-Release Support:** Provide ongoing support and updates for your game after release to address bug fixes, performance improvements, and feature enhancements. Monitor user feedback and reviews on each platform and respond to player inquiries, suggestions, and issues promptly.

By following these steps, you can successfully deploy your C++ game on multiple platforms, reach a wider audience, and maximize the potential for success in the competitive gaming market.

Sample Game Project

Let's develop a classic brick game in C++, inspired by games like Breakout or Arkanoid.

Introduction: Welcome to the world of classic brick-breaking fun! In our game, players control a paddle at the bottom of the screen, bouncing a ball to break bricks stacked at the top. With precise control and quick reflexes, players must clear each level by breaking all the bricks while preventing the ball from falling off the screen. Get ready for addictive gameplay, challenging levels, and nostalgic fun in this timeless arcade experience.

Game Plan:

1. **Setting the Stage:**

- Create a simple game window with a paddle, ball, and bricks.
- Design multiple levels with varying brick layouts and difficulty levels.
- Implement collision detection between the ball, paddle, and bricks.

1. **Gameplay Mechanics:**

- Enable player-controlled paddle movement using keyboard or mouse inputs.
- Implement ball movement and collision physics to bounce off walls, paddle, and bricks.

- Track score, lives, and level progression to provide feedback and challenge to players.

1. **User Interface:**

- Design a minimalistic user interface with score display, lives remaining, and level indicator.
- Include game over and level completion screens with options to restart or quit the game.
- Provide visual and audio feedback for paddle movement, ball collisions, and brick destruction.

1. **Art and Sound Design:**

- Create colorful brick sprites with different shapes, sizes, and colors.
- Design animations for ball movement, paddle interaction, and brick destruction.
- Compose retro-inspired sound effects and background music to enhance the arcade atmosphere and gameplay experience.

Now, let's start coding the game, beginning with setting up the game window and initializing the game engine. I have used comments to explain every section of the game. Feel free to modify the code to your expectation.

```cpp
#include <SFML/Graphics.hpp>

// Constants
const int WINDOW_WIDTH = 800;
const int WINDOW_HEIGHT = 600;
const int PADDLE_WIDTH = 100;
const int PADDLE_HEIGHT = 20;
const int PADDLE_SPEED = 5;
const int BALL_RADIUS = 10;
const int BALL_SPEED = 5;
```

```cpp
const int BRICK_WIDTH = 80;
const int BRICK_HEIGHT = 30;
const int NUM_BRICKS_X = 10;
const int NUM_BRICKS_Y = 5;

// Function to handle collision between two rectangles
bool isIntersecting(const sf::RectangleShape& rect1, const
sf::RectangleShape& rect2) {
    return
    rect1.getGlobalBounds().intersects(rect2.getGlobalBounds());
}

int main() {
    // Create the game window
    sf::RenderWindow window(sf::VideoMode(WINDOW_WIDTH,
    WINDOW_HEIGHT), "Brick Breaker");

    // Create the paddle
    sf::RectangleShape paddle(sf::Vector2f(PADDLE_WIDTH,
    PADDLE_HEIGHT));
    paddle.setFillColor(sf::Color::White);
    paddle.setPosition((WINDOW_WIDTH - PADDLE_WIDTH) / 2,
    WINDOW_HEIGHT - PADDLE_HEIGHT - 20);

    // Create the ball
    sf::CircleShape ball(BALL_RADIUS);
    ball.setFillColor(sf::Color::White);
    ball.setPosition((WINDOW_WIDTH - BALL_RADIUS) / 2,
    (WINDOW_HEIGHT - BALL_RADIUS) / 2);
    sf::Vector2f ballVelocity(BALL_SPEED, BALL_SPEED);

    // Create the bricks
    sf::RectangleShape bricks[NUM_BRICKS_X][NUM_BRICKS_Y];
    for (int i = 0; i < NUM_BRICKS_X; ++i) {
        for (int j = 0; j < NUM_BRICKS_Y; ++j) {
            bricks[i][j] =
            sf::RectangleShape(sf::Vector2f(BRICK_WIDTH,
            BRICK_HEIGHT));
            bricks[i][j].setFillColor(sf::Color::Green);
            bricks[i][j].setPosition(i * (BRICK_WIDTH + 5), j *
```

```cpp
        (BRICK_HEIGHT + 5) + 50);
    }
}


// Game loop
while (window.isOpen()) {
    // Handle events
    sf::Event event;
    while (window.pollEvent(event)) {
        if (event.type == sf::Event::Closed)
            window.close();
    }


    // Move the paddle
    if (sf::Keyboard::isKeyPressed(sf::Keyboard::Left) &&
    paddle.getPosition().x > 0) {
        paddle.move(-PADDLE_SPEED, 0);
    }
    if (sf::Keyboard::isKeyPressed(sf::Keyboard::Right) &&
    paddle.getPosition().x < WINDOW_WIDTH - PADDLE_WIDTH) {
        paddle.move(PADDLE_SPEED, 0);
    }


    // Move the ball
    ball.move(ballVelocity);


    // Check collision with window boundaries
    if (ball.getPosition().x < 0 || ball.getPosition().x >
    WINDOW_WIDTH - BALL_RADIUS) {
        ballVelocity.x = -ballVelocity.x;
    }
    if (ball.getPosition().y < 0 || ball.getPosition().y >
    WINDOW_HEIGHT - BALL_RADIUS) {
        ballVelocity.y = -ballVelocity.y;
    }


    // Check collision with paddle
    if (isIntersecting(ball, paddle)) {
        ballVelocity.y = -ballVelocity.y;
    }
```

```cpp
        // Check collision with bricks
        for (int i = 0; i < NUM_BRICKS_X; ++i) {
            for (int j = 0; j < NUM_BRICKS_Y; ++j) {
                if (bricks[i][j].getFillColor() !=
                sf::Color::Transparent && isIntersecting(ball,
                bricks[i][j])) {
                    bricks[i][j].setFillColor(sf::Color::Transparent);
                    ballVelocity.y = -ballVelocity.y;
                }
            }
        }

        // Clear the window
        window.clear(sf::Color::Black);

        // Draw the paddle
        window.draw(paddle);

        // Draw the ball
        window.draw(ball);

        // Draw the bricks
        for (int i = 0; i < NUM_BRICKS_X; ++i) {
            for (int j = 0; j < NUM_BRICKS_Y; ++j) {
                if (bricks[i][j].getFillColor() !=
                sf::Color::Transparent) {
                    window.draw(bricks[i][j]);
                }
            }
        }

        // Display the window
        window.display();
    }

    return 0;
}
```

Explanation:

- We include the SFML library for graphics and window management.
- We define constants for window dimensions, paddle and ball properties, and brick layout.
- In the **main** function, we create a **RenderWindow** object named **window** with the specified dimensions and title.
- We create the paddle and ball shapes using **RectangleShape** and **CircleShape** objects and set their properties such as color, size, and position.
- We create a 2D array of **RectangleShape** objects for the bricks and initialize their positions and colors.
- Inside the game loop, we handle window events such as closing the window.
- We move the paddle left or right based on keyboard input and prevent it from going out of bounds.
- We move the ball and handle collisions with window boundaries, paddle, and bricks.
- We clear the window, draw the game elements (paddle, ball, bricks), and display the window to the player.
- Finally, we return 0 to indicate successful program execution.

This code provides a basic framework for a brick game, including paddle movement, ball physics, and brick collision detection. You can further expand and enhance the game by adding features such as scoring, levels, power-ups, and sound effects.

Hope you Enjoyed reading this book!

References

Adams, J. (2019). *SFML Game Development by Example.* Packt Publishing.

Dawson, M. (2018). *Beginning C++ Game Programming.* Packt Publishing.

Gregory, J. (2017). *Game Engine Architecture.* CRC Press.

Lamothe, A. (2013). *Tricks of the Windows Game Programming Gurus.* Sams Publishing.

McShaffry, M. (2005). *Game Coding Complete.* Paraglyph Press.

Polack-Wahl, J. (2019). *The C++ Standard Library.* Addison-Wesley Professional.

Rabin, S. (2019). *Introduction to Game Development.* CRC Press.

Sutherland, W. (2016). *SFML Game Development.* Packt Publishing.

Tanaka, M. (2017). *Beginning C++ Game Programming.* Apress.

Van Verth, J. (2017). *Essential Mathematics for Games and Interactive Applications.* CRC Press.

About the Author

Jarrel E. is a college teacher who teaches computer programming courses. He has been writing programs since he was 15 years old. Jarrel currently focuses on writing software that addresses inefficiencies in education and brings the benefits of open source software to the field of education. In his spare time, he enjoys climbing mountains and spending time with his family.

Also by Jarrel E.

Crafting Games with Python: From Basics to Brilliance
Crafting Games with Python: From Basics to Brilliance stands as an exhaustive guide, ushering aspiring game developers through a comprehensive journey from fundamental concepts to mastery in Python game development. Here's a detailed overview:

C++ for Game Developers: Building Scalable and Robust Gaming Applications

Embark on a comprehensive journey through the intricacies of C++ for game development with this expertly crafted guide. Tailored for advanced programmers, this book serves as a definitive resource for building scalable and robust gaming applications.